ANYONE CAN WHISTLE

❀ ❀ ❀

A Musical Fable

Book by

Arthur Laurents

Music and Lyrics by

Stephen Sondheim

A Carl Peek Book
LEON AMIEL PUBLISHER
New York, New York

A NOTE FROM THE PUBLISHER

Publishing trade editions of Broadway shows is a precarious business at best; reissuing *Anyone Can Whistle* after 12 years and only 9 performances is downright crazy (or so I've been told). But there are some things worth saving: *Anyone Can Whistle* is one—a modern classic from the American musical stage. So a note of thanks to those people who made this edition possible: Mike Stapleton, whose idea it was; Herman Krawitz of Yale University who located the seemingly only extant copy of the original edition; C. V. Wimpfheimer of Random House; Nancy Stark of Doubleday's Fireside Theatre; Charles Schlessiger of Brandt & Brandt; Flora Roberts; Lee Snider of Chappell Music; Terry Hammond, who first played me the score; Joseph Abeles; Bill Konecky, Curtis Holsapple, Roy Jensen and David Smith, all of whom contributed to the final product. And special thanks to Leon Amiel whose concern for artistic achievement in all fields made the republication of this book a reality.

—*Carl Peek*

Introduction

When *Anyone Can Whistle* opened on Broadway on April 4, 1964, Whitney Bolton of the *Morning Telegraph* prophesied:

"If *Anyone Can Whistle* is a success, the American musical theatre will have advanced itself and prepared the way for further breakdown of now old and worn techniques and points of view. If it is not a success, we sink back into the old formula method and must wait for the breakthrough.

"Arthur Laurents takes a scalpel to a flourish of our illusions and cuts away the fat. He puts before us the credo that in this day to be mad is to be sane, to be insane is to be healthy and in proper mental frame for this day. We live, in short, in crazy times and it is better for the individual to be somewhat daft and, thus, meet craze with craze.

"To all concerned, top and bottom, a thank you for trying, a thank you for wanting to elevate the American musical theatre to new standards of intellect. Let no one concerned be discouraged.

"The American musical theatre is less ponderous and ridiculous today because of *Anyone Can Whistle*, no matter what its fate."

Its fate was not a bright one. For despite the efforts of a few particularly insightful critics, the majority were outraged at the violation of traditional musical comedy forms. With the wrath of the Broadway establishment raining upon its head, *Anyone Can Whistle* succumbed to a premature demise after but nine performances at a loss of its entire $350,000 investment (including financial backing by four musical theatre greats: Irving Berlin, Frank Loesser, Richard Rodgers, and Jule Styne, who had faith in the project).

Here, at last, was a truly new musical, in a theatre full of so-called new musicals, which were, in actuality, musical adaptations of other sources usually best left unmusicalized; a musical that incorporated scathing satire with sly subtlety; a lively but literate libretto with a wise and witty score. *Anyone Can Whistle* was the marriage of musical comedy with theatre of the absurd, consummated cleverly and exhilaratingly executed.

Martin Gottfried of *Women's Wear Daily* exulted:

"It's not simply that *Anyone Can Whistle* is a brilliantly inventive musical . . . It is a ringingly bright shout for individuality and because it is so individual itself, it is whole, it is fresh, it is new, and it is perfectly wonderful.

"Thank heavens that there still are adults in the theatre. And that they are willing to assume that their audience is adult, too. Mr. Laurents has written a book that fairly glitters with fey wit and mature insight . . . His humor does not condescend with cheap broadness, his characters do not insult with nice-guy, sweet girl superficiality. He has not written a simple story geared for handy songs and dances. Nor has Mr. Sondheim provided simpleminded music for it. Here are songs that combine musical sophistication with theatrical flair. At once melodic and interesting, they easily represent the finest Broadway composing in years.

"This is—you must know by now—a real original, and that is just what it is asking us to be if we want to be alive at all.

"*Anyone Can Whistle* is as alive as it is telling everybody to be and that makes it both important and exciting."

Although *Anyone Can Whistle* was short-lived on Broadway, it has had more influence on the development of the contemporary musical theatre than dozens of more commercially successful shows. It helped sow the seeds of discontent with a once fresh and vital art form that had begun to atrophy with convention, to shine a light through a glut of tuneful but essentially mindless mediocrities that littered the musical stages of the 1960's. It posed new challenges to librettists who made money by stringing songs to one-liners and writing caricatures instead of characters. And it began to establish a criterion on which a musical score should be based: Is a good score just something you can hum on your way out of the theatre? Or shouldn't it accomplish some development of tone, or characterization?

Many of these dilemmas were confronted and conquered in the later concept musicals devised by Stephen Sondheim and producer, Harold Prince; landmarks that include *Company* (1970), *Follies* (1971), *A Little Night Music* (1973), and *Pacific Overtures* (1976). Certainly, *Anyone Can Whistle* definitively marks the turning point in Mr. Sondheim's musical direction.

Mr. Laurents' and Mr. Sondheim's contributions notwithstanding, *Anyone Can Whistle* had other assets, including remarkable sets by William and Jean Eckart, clever costumes by Theoni V. Aldredge and evocative lighting by Jules Fisher. Arthur Laurents directed the production himself, a particularly uncommon accomplishment in the incorporation of the creative and interpretative artist, with Herbert Ross supplying truly memorable and undeniably innovative dance numbers. The show was also blessed with performances of pin-point accuracy and sincerity by Lee Remick as Nurse Fay Apple, and Harry Guardino as J. Bowden Hapgood. Angela Lansbury made her musical comedy debut as Cora Hoover Hooper, an important first step toward a brilliantly successful career in that medium which would include a third Tony Award as star of the 1974 revival of the Arthur Laurents-Stephen Sondheim-Jule Styne musical, *Gypsy*.

Although *Anyone Can Whistle* did not win popular acclaim, or even acceptance during its brief lifetime, it has endured to become that rare phenomenon, a cult musical (By definition, a musical of distinguished merit which enjoys continued, albeit limited popularity despite an abbreviated commercial run. *Candide* is another example, unique in that the perseverance of its cult inspired a major revival.), whose devotees can savor this little known masterpiece on the original cast album (recorded posthumously, following the show's closing on April 11, 1964) and now in this new published edition.

—*David Smith*

MUSICAL NUMBERS

ACT ONE

"I'M LIKE THE BLUEBIRD"	Cookies
"ME AND MY TOWN"	Cora and The Boys
"MIRACLE SONG"	Cora, Cooley, Townspeople, Tourists, and Pilgrims
"SIMPLE"	Hapgood and Company

ACT TWO

"A-I MARCH"	Company
"COME PLAY WITH ME"	Fay, Hapgood and The Boys
"ANYONE CAN WHISTLE"	Fay
"A PARADE IN TOWN"	Cora
"EVERYBODY SAYS DON'T"	Hapgood

ACT THREE

"I'VE GOT YOU TO LEAN ON"	Cora, Schub, Cooley, Magruder and The Boys
"SEE WHAT IT GETS YOU"	Fay
"THE COOKIE CHASE"	Cora, Fay and Company
"WITH SO LITTLE TO BE SURE OF"	Fay and Hapgood

ANYONE CAN WHISTLE *was first presented by Kermit Bloom-garden and Diana Krasny at the Majestic Theatre, New York City, on April 4, 1964, with the following cast:*

(In order of appearance)

SANDWICH MAN	Jeff Killion
BABY JOAN	Jeanne Tanzy
MRS. SCHROEDER	Peg Murray
TREASURER COOLEY	Arnold Soboloff
CHIEF MAGRUDER	James Frawley
COMPTROLLER SCHUB	Gabriel Dell
CORA HOOVER HOOPER	Angela Lansbury
THE BOYS	Sterling Clark, Harvey Evans, Larry Roquemore, Tucker Smith
FAY APPLE	Lee Remick
J. BOWDEN HAPGOOD	Harry Guardino
DR. DETMOLD	Don Doherty
GEORGE	Larry Roquemore
JUNE	Janet Hayes
JOHN	Harvey Evans
MARTIN	Lester Wilson
OLD LADY	Eleonore Treiber
TELEGRAPH BOY	Alan Johnson
OSGOOD	Georgia Creighton

and

Susan Borree, Georgia Creighton, Janet Hayes, Bettye Jenkins, Patricia Kelly, Barbara Lang, Paula Lloyd, Barbara Monte, Odette Phillips, Hanne-Marie Reiner, Eleonore Treiber, Sterling Clark, Eugene Edwards, Harvey Evans, Dick Ensslen, Loren Hightower, Alan Johnson, Jeff Killion, Jack Murray, William Reilly, Larry Roquemore, Tucker Smith, Don Stewart, Lester Wilson *as*

COOKIES, NURSES, DEPUTIES, TOWNSPEOPLE, PILGRIMS AND TOURISTS.

Directed by Arthur Laurents
Dances and Musical Numbers Staged by Herbert Ross
Scenery designed by William and Jean Eckart
Costumes by Theoni V. Aldredge
Lighting by Jules Fisher
Orchestrations by Don Walker
Vocal Arrangements and Musical Direction by
Herbert Green
Dance Arrangements by Betty Walberg
Associate Producer: Arlene Sellers

ACT ONE

The curtain rises to a burst of circus-like music on the main square of a town. The colors are gay, exaggerated; the look is rather Pop Art cockeyed. At one side is the entrance to City Hall; at the other, the entrance to the Hotel Superbe. As the music softens to a jazzy pulse underneath, from offstage comes a humorously folksy voice.

NARRATOR

This is our setting: the main square of a town. This town manufactured a product that never wore out. This is what happened. (*Immediately, a building falls down; a crack appears in the facade of City Hall; the Hotel Superbe's sign teeters at an angle; and signs fly in reading* CLOSED, VACANCY *and* HELP!) These are some of the citizens of the town. (*A group of people in stylized rags and clown wigs lope on and glare at the audience*) Believe it or not, they once looked as good as you. Maybe better. It'll take a miracle to make them human again—but we may be able to produce one.

> (*The music changes and a group of pleasantly dressed, smiling people enters, led by a slightly tipsy nurse. These people are* COOKIES *and they sing*)

COOKIES

I'm like the bluebird.
I should worry, I should care.
I should be a millionaire.
I'm like the blue—
> (*In mid-phrase, they cut off and freeze with smiles on their faces*)

NARRATOR

There *is* one place in this town that's still doing business: that's The Cookie Jar: a sanitarium for the socially pressured. Those Cookies look as good as you. Maybe better. (*The* COOKIES *wave*) Our heroine is the head nurse. No, not that nurse. (*She hiccups silently*) She drinks. Our girl won't be along for eleven minutes. Run along, Cookies. (*They exit to the "Bluebird March"*) Now to return to this broken-down town.

> (*The music takes on a strong jazz rhythm as the* TOWNSPEOPLE *do vaudeville-like dance movements and chant with great glee*)

TOWNSPEOPLE

Help! Help!
Hungry! Hungry!
Poor! Poor!
RESIGN!

> (*On this last, they turn to City Hall and freeze with upraised fists*)

NARRATOR

Where is all the town's money? Where it usually is: in City Hall.

> (*A burst of music and out of City Hall snakes a thin man with a fistful of money. He leers at the money and freezes as one of the townsmen who has been carrying a sandwich board reading* DOWN WITH THE ADMINISTRATION *flips over a card so that the sign now reads* DOWN WITH TREASURER COOLEY)

SANDWICH MAN

Down With Treasurer Cooley!

NARRATOR

That snoop's got some of it.

(*The* TOWNSPEOPLE *hiss as there is another burst of music and a hulking, uniformed man comes out of City Hall. He has a stupid grin on his face which changes to a pout as he holds out his hand for money and* COOLEY *merely gives him one bill. Everyone freezes but the* SANDWICH MAN *who flips his card over to read*)

SANDWICH MAN

Down With Chief of Police Magruder!

NARRATOR

That moron's got some of it.

(*The people growl angrily as there is another burst of music and a foppish Edwardian-looking man comes out of City Hall. He takes all the money from both* COOLEY *and* MAGRUDER *as, again, everybody freezes except the* SANDWICH MAN *for*)

SANDWICH MAN

Down With Comptroller Schub!

NARRATOR

That operator's got some of it—but his eye is on the main chunk. And there it is! (*An enormous fanfare: the crowd boos;* SCHUB, COOLEY *and* MAGRUDER *move to one side; and on comes an attractive lady, glittering madly with too many diamonds. Her name is* CORA HOOVER HOOPER *and she is carried Cleopatra-like on a litter, by four* PAGE BOYS) Cora Hoover Hooper: the Mayoress. They ought to throw rocks at her.

(*And the people do! They snarl, boo, shout curses;
the* SANDWICH MAN *flips his sign to read* DOWN
WITH THE MAYORESS. *But none of this disturbs*
CORA *who descends from her litter with great hauteur.
The* BOYS *carry the litter off, the columned facade of
City Hall slides on behind her and, midst the last of
the flying rocks, she sings*)

CORA

Everyone hates me—yes, yes—
Being the Mayor—ess, yes.
All of the peasants
Throw rocks in my presence
Which causes me nervous distress, yes.
Oooh Oooooooooooh, Oooh-ooh Oooooooooh.
        (*During this rather torch-singer-like moan, the last
        peasant straggles off*)
Me and my town, battered about,
Everyone in it would like to get out.
Me and my town,
We just wanna be loved!
Stores are for rent, theatres are dark,
Grass on the sidewalks but not in the park,
Me and my town—me and my town—
We just wanna be loved!
        (*Behind her now some of the people appear doing a
        shuffling dance step*)
The people are starving,
So they sleep the day through.
My poor little people,
What can they do?

TOWNSPEOPLE

Boo!

CORA

Who asked you?
    (*She glares at them; they run off*)
Come on the train, come on the bus,
Somebody please buy a ticket to us.
Hurry on down—
We need a little renown.
Love me,
Love my
Town!
Ooohhh—ooooohhhhh—ooooooooooooohhhhhhhhhhhh!
    (*Four* BOYS *appear suddenly out of nowhere: the
    number becomes a jazzy parody of a night-club num-
    ber*)

BOYS

Hi there, Cora. What's new?

CORA

The bank went bust and I'm feeling blue.

BOYS

And who took over the bankruptcy?

CORA

Me, boys, me!

BOYS

Si, si!

CORA

Me, boys, me!

BOYS

Tell us, Cora, how you are.

CORA

I just got back from the reservoir.

BOYS

And what's the state of the water supply?

CORA

Dry, boys, dry!

BOYS

My, my!

CORA

Dry, boys, dry!

BOYS

Ay, ay!

(*The music stops and they begin a clapping accompaniment*)

CORA

A lady has responsibilities . . .

BOYS

Responsibilities . . .

CORA

And civic pride.

BOYS

Civic pride!

CORA

Well, I look around and what do I see? I see *no* crops.

BOYS

No crops.

CORA

I see *no* business.

BOYS

No business.

CORA

To the North, to the South,
    Only hoof-and-mouth!
To the East, to the West,
    No Community Chest!

CORA *and* BOYS

I see a terrible depression all over the town—
Oh, a terrible depression,
Yes, a terrible depression,

CORA

What a terrible depression
And I'm so depressed I can hardly talk on the phone.
I feel all alone.

CORA *and* BOYS

But a lady has responsibilities—

BOYS

Responsibilities—

CORA

To all my poor! starving! miserable! dirty! dreary!
    depressing!
Peasants!

ALL

Peasants! Ugh!

CORA

But a lady has responsibilities—

BOYS

Responsibilities—

CORA

To try to be
Popular with the populace.

BOYS

She's unpopular with the populace!

CORA *and* BOYS

Unpopular with the populace, unpopular with the
populace . . .
> (*Music sneaks back in under* CORA)

CORA

Last week a flood, this week a drought,
Even the locusts want to get out,
But me and my town, we never pout,
We just wanna be loved!

BOYS

A friendship is lovely
And a courtship sublime,
But give her a township

CORA

Township!
Every time!

CORA *and* BOYS

What'll we do, me and my town?
Gotta do something or we're gonna drown!
> (*In a strut*)
Give me my coat,
Give me my crown,
Give me your vote
And hurry on down.

CORA

Show me how much you think *of* me!

ALL

Love me,
Love my
Town!

> (*On the last close-harmony held note, they are strutting across the stage towards an exit.* CORA *gives the last boy a playful little shove so that she can take the bow for the number alone—which she does. She then beckons them to return with her litter as* SCHUB *enters*)

SCHUB

My dear Madam Mayor—

CORA

I'm in the depths of positive despair.
> (*She sinks onto the litter*)

SCHUB

Ah now, Cora, you need to relax.

CORA

I need a miracle, that's what I need.

SCHUB

Why don't we dine together this evening? (*The* BOYS *glare at him and lift* CORA *and the litter into the air*) My house at eight. Or your house. It makes no difference. I'll be at your house at seven.

CORA

You will not! You'll just try to talk me into re-opening my

great big enormous factory. I know that's why you got me
elected, you and Magruder and Cooley—where is that little
snoop?

COOLEY

(*Who has sneaked on and been listening under the litter*)
At your service, Sister Hoover Hooper.

CORA

A fine City Treasurer you are!

COOLEY

I thank you.

CORA

My desk is littered with bills. Pay them.

COOLEY

With what, Sister?

CORA

Ingenuity, Brother, ingenuity.

COOLEY

By the day after tomorrow, this town will be bankrupt!

SCHUB

We had thought of selling it—

COOLEY

But only you, Sister, could afford to buy it.

CORA

Count—me—out—and—(*To her* BOYS) Put—me—down!

SCHUB

Now Cora, I have conjured up a plan to save your town.

CORA

(*To the* BOYS)
Home! (*They leave with the litter; to* SCHUB) You and
your plans! Another World's Fair? Another Peer Gynt Festival? Why can't you think of a plan that will work?

SCHUB

This one will: it's unethical.

COOLEY

Highly.

CORA

(*Suddenly singing* a capella)
I didn't hear it! Don't tell me! (*She speaks sharply*) But do
it! Now: how much is it going to cost?

SCHUB

Nothing.

CORA

I love it.

SCHUB

All it needs is Baby Joan.

CORA

Baby Joan? Baby Joan Schroeder??

COOLEY

Don't worry. I'll get her.
(*He goes*)

CORA

Get her for what? Schub, you genius, what *is* this plan?

SCHUB

(*Fondling her*)
Let me surprise you, dear lady.

CORA

Oh, I adore surprises!

SCHUB

Then prepare for prosperity and meet me at The Rock as soon as you can.

CORA

I'll change and be there in no time! (SCHUB *kisses her hand and exits. Music strikes up and the four* BOYS *dance on with a change of costume and jewelry for* CORA. *At the same time, the scenery is changing: City Hall is sliding off as a great rock slides on. But before everything can be set in place,* CORA, *who has been struggling to get a glove on, holds up her hand for everything to stop. And it does, both music and scenery. She hums cheerfully until she gets the glove on, then beckons with her hand for the music and scene change to resume.*

*They do, speedily; the lights come up and she looks around,
singing* a capella) *Schub! Comptroller Schub!*
    (*At the same time, there is yelling from offstage and a
rather mad-looking woman in rags enters*)

MRS. SCHROEDER

Baby Joan! Baby Joan!

CORA

SCHUB!

MRS. SCHROEDER

BABY JOAN!

CORA

Schroeder, have you lost that child of yours again? I
thought I told you to put a bell around her neck.

MRS. SCHROEDER

You take care of your town, I'll take care of my kid. BABY
JOAN!

CORA

SCHUB! COMPTROLLER—
    (*Both ladies stop dead. A weird looking little brat of 7
or 8—*BABY JOAN—*has been shoved on by* COOLEY
who then scurries behind the rock. BABY JOAN *shuts
her eyes, extends her hands, begins to head for the
rock, uttering strange moans*)

MRS. SCHROEDER

(*In disgust*)

Oh, Baby Joan!

CORA

Is she in some sort of a trance?

MRS. SCHROEDER

No. (BABY JOAN *now nestles down and begins to lick the rock*) She's thirsty.

CORA

And in a trance.

MRS. SCHROEDER

Have it your way.

CORA

Don't you tell me this town is even out of water! If you were any kind of a decent mother, you'd take that child home!

MRS. SCHROEDER

Why? All she needs is a good belt in the—
    (*But suddenly there is an enormous spurt of water from the rock and a spurt of music from the orchestra*)

CORA

(*A whisper*)

Schroeder—

MRS. SCHROEDER

Your Honor—

CORA

(*Clutching her*)

Schroeder!

MRS. SCHROEDER

Your Honor! It's—it's a miracle!

CORA

It's a what?

MRS. SCHROEDER

A miracle! It's a miracle!

CORA

(*Looks at the water, then back at* MRS. SCHROEDER)
You know, you're absolutely right! It's a miracle! I'm saved!
(*At this,* BABY JOAN *runs to the footlights, curtseys
modestly, then returns to the rock where she stands
in an angelic pose as religious music starts.* TOWNS-
PEOPLE *come running on, and* COOLEY *appears from
behind the rock to make sure the "miracle" is working
and* BABY JOAN *is behaving*)

TOWNSPEOPLE

(*Chanting*)

Ah! Ah!

MRS. SCHROEDER

(*Sings*)

It's a sign! It's a sign!

CORA

And it's mine!

MRS. SCHROEDER

It's a shrine ! It's a shrine!

CORA

And it's mine!
It's a gold mine!
And it's all mine!

TOWNSPEOPLE

It's a sign!
It's a shrine!
See it shine!

CORA

And it's holier than thine!

CORA, COOLEY, MRS. SCHROEDER, TOWNSPEOPLE

There's water in a lake,
Water in a river,
Water in the deep blue sea.
But water in a rock—Lord! That's a miracle!

CORA *and* COOLEY

Who's got the miracle? We!

ALL

There's water that you part,
Water that you walk on,

Water that you turn to wine!
But water from a rock—Lord! What a miracle!
This is a miracle that's divine,
Truly divine!

CORA

Really *divine!*

CORA, COOLEY, MRS. SCHROEDER

The Lord said, "Let there be water,"
The Lord said, "Turn on the font!"
Lord said, "Let there be pilgrims
And let 'em all think whatever they want."

ALL

Blessed be the child,
Blessed be the tourist,
Blessed is its own reward.

COOLEY

Water is a boon, we'll soon be in clover!

CORA

Better issue stock, my rock runneth over!

ALL

Glory Hallelu,
You finally came through,
And thank you, Lord!
Our faith is restored!
Thank you, Lord!
      (*And now* PILGRIMS *enter—all types from all over*)

CORA

Come all ye pilgrims!

TOWNSPEOPLE

Hail the miracle!

CORA

See ye the wondrous sight!

TOWNSPEOPLE

Hail the miracle, praise the miracle!

CORA

Take ye the bus tonight.

TOWNSPEOPLE

There's a miracle that's happening in this town.

CORA

If you want to see a miracle, then hurry on down!

COOLEY

Come all ye pilgrims!

TOWNSPEOPLE

Hail the miracle.

COOLEY

Hear ye the joyful bells!

TOWNSPEOPLE

Hail the miracle.

COOLEY

Fill ye the new motels!

TOWNSPEOPLE

It's a miracle that's going to change your life.

COOLEY

Come along and see the miracle and bring the wife!

TOWNSPEOPLE

There's a miracle that's happening in this town
And you'll never have to worry if you hurry on down.
There's a miracle that's going to change your life!
Come along and see the miracle and bring the wife!

CORA

(*Like a revival meeting leader, to the* PILGRIMS)
Are you looking for hope?

TOWNSPEOPLE

Looking for hope . . .

CORA

Hoping for an answer?

TOWNSPEOPLE

Hoping for an answer . . .

CORA

New life.

TOWNSPEOPLE

New life . . .

CORA

True happiness.

TOWNSPEOPLE

True happiness . . .

CORA

Come.

> (There is a murmuring babble from the PILGRIMS,
> not unlike that heard in crowd-filled cathedrals,
> which culminates in a single distinct word)

PILGRIMS

(Murmur)

Help.

CORA

Come and take the waters for a modest fee.
Come and take the waters and feel new.
Come and take the waters and with luck you'll be
Anything whatever except you.

> (During this, the PILGRIMS take offerings to BABY
> JOAN on the rock: jewelry, wrist watches, cameras,
> money, suitcases, anything. And anything, particu-
> larly money, is solemnly accepted and raked in by
> COOLEY. Then the PILGRIMS extend their hands and
> murmur)

PILGRIMS

Comfort.

TOWNSPEOPLE

Come and take the waters with humility.
Come and take the waters and feel new.

CORA

Come and take the waters and with luck you'll be
Happy and successful!

PILGRIMS *and* TOWNSPEOPLE

Happy and successful!

CORA

Liked and loved and beautiful and perfect!

PILGRIMS *and* TOWNSPEOPLE

Beautiful and perfect!

CORA

Healthy, rich, handsome, independent,
Wise, adjusted and secure and athletic!

PILGRIMS

(*With wild excitement, they babble, rush to the rock, and call
out, pointing in different directions:*)
Rainbow; rainbow; rainbow; rainbow! (*And now they all
rush forward and pointing here, there, everywhere, all scream
in one burst of ecstasy*) RAINBOW! ! !
      (*The music roars over them as they go really wild:
dashing up the rock to the water, throwing water over*

each other, kissing the rock, rolling on the ground, kissing BABY JOAN's *feet. This last is a bit disconcerting to* CORA *who, with* MRS. SCHROEDER, *is trying to get* BABY JOAN *into one of her better nightgowns. At the same time flowers appear, buildings straighten and the town gets a look of prosperity)*

ALL

The Lord said, "Let there be water!"
The Lord said, "Turn on the font!"
Lord said, "Let ye be what ye want!"
Our troubles are over!
OUR TROUBLES ARE OVER! ! !
Look upon the gift and lift up your chin now!

CORA *and* COOLEY

Look upon the boom—no room at the Inn now!

ALL

Glory Hallelu,
Our problems are through,
And thank you, Lord!
Thank you, Lord!
　　*(*CORA *is hoisted on the shoulders of admirers and over the final note, shrieks)*

CORA

THEY LOVE ME! ! !
　　(Jubilant music and singing resume as the rock revolves and we see what is behind it: a cave in the interior in which MAGRUDER *is enthusiastically working a long-handled water pump.* COOLEY *and* SCHUB *rush in;* SCHUB *begins to fiddle with some electrical wires)*

COOLEY

More and more pilgrims!

SCHUB

It's an absolute gold rush!

COOLEY

As long as the flock is happy, Brethren—they spend.
(*Helps* MAGRUDER *pump*)

SCHUB

Which reminds me: I got Madam Schroeder to sign three exclusive contracts for the manufacture of Baby Joan statuettes: small, medium and life-size.

COOLEY

To be sold, Brother Schub—

SCHUB

Exclusively in Cooley stores—

MAGRUDER

Providing a license is obtained—

SCHUB

From the Chief of Police. Subject to the approval of the Comptroller and payable to the Treasurer.

COOLEY

(*Hands to heaven*)
Sing out the truth!

SCHUB

Keep pumping. If either of you cretins knew anything about electricity, I'd have had this working automatically ages—

CORA

(*Off—singing* a capella)
Schub! Comptroller Schub!

MAGRUDER

We're lost!

SCHUB

Keep pumping!

CORA

(*Off*)
Schub! Comptroller—(*They freeze as she bursts in the door, carrying an armful of roses*)—Schub . . .

SCHUB

It's a nonsectarian miracle, Cora.

CORA

(A capella)
I didn't hear it! Don't tell me! (*Then speaks sharply*) But do it. (*The pumping resumes*) And keep doing it.

SCHUB

You are a mayor and a lady. Seven-thirty, my house.

CORA

(*Sadly*)

Ah me. On my wedding day, the late Harvey Hoover Hooper gave me a triple strand of pearls. The next morning —it was my fourteenth birthday—I took them to a jeweler.

SCHUB

For safekeeping.

CORA

No, for appraisal. My pearls were cultured. (*Dumps the roses on* SCHUB) I keep hoping for something real.

SCHUB

Madame, a little while ago, they wanted to run you out of town. Now they want to run you for governor. If that isn't a real miracle, nothing is.

CORA

Ha ha ha ha! You're right. (*Yanks the roses back*) I shall proceed with my plan to re-open my factory as a bottling plant for Miracle Water. Keep pumping. And don't get tired.

SCHUB

One brilliant moment, dear lady. I'm about ready to hook up the electricity.

CORA

Electricity! Oh, Schub-chen! It's like the opening of the Suez Canal and I'm Queen Whatever-her-name-was! I knight all of you! (*A rose to each of them*) A miracle is a miracle if it works like a miracle! All those poor sweet pilgrims standing in

line: I never knew so many would pay so much for new lives.
And I never dreamed it would all happen in my reign!

SCHUB

Dinner, your Highness?

CORA

Seven-thirty, my house.
(*A last rose to him, and she exits*)

MAGRUDER

Ten to one, she's not gonna cut us in on her water.

COOLEY

Feareth not, Brother. We shall sell tickets to ours!

SCHUB

Stop pumping! . . . Stand back! . . . And pray. (*He goes
to a switch*) If this works, it *will* be a miracle.
  (*He throws the switch. Nothing happens. In disgust,
  he removes a rose stuck in the pump. A moment, then
  the handle starts pumping, slowly, awkwardly to
  music, faster, then cheerfully and happily.* COOLEY
  and MAGRUDER *yell ecstatically and begin to dance
  in time to the pumping as the rock revolves again, and
  we see the "miracle" and a longer line of* PILGRIMS
  waiting for it. BABY JOAN *is sitting on top of the rock,
  extending her hand for* PILGRIMS *to kiss—and then
  opening it for a fee which they pay her and which she
  puts in a tin can.* COOLEY *now has a fat roll of red
  movie-theatre tickets which he is selling*)

COOLEY

Step up, brethren and sistren! Get your tickets!

MAGRUDER

Buy your blessings!

COOLEY

Count your blessings, buy your tickets.

MAGRUDER

Yeah, step right up! Only one blessing per pilgrim per ticket!

COOLEY

Step up! Special discount for minority groups!
(*As they continue, the music changes and the "Blue-bird Song" is heard as a line of* COOKIES *marches on, led by their young, pretty head nurse,* FAY APPLE. *The music stops as she stops, leaving her* COOKIES *in a line behind her, downstage of and parallel to the line of* PILGRIMS. FAY *takes a step and looks coldly at the rock*)

FAY

So that's it.

COOLEY

Yes, ma'am, Sister Nurse Apple!

FAY

Forty-nine tickets, please.

COOLEY

Forty-nine?

FAY

We have forty-nine patients in Dr. Detmold's Cookie Jar! I want a ticket for each and every Cookie.

COOKIES

Hooray!

COOLEY

Sing out the truth!

FAY

Baby Joan Schroeder, you come right down off that wet rock!

BABY JOAN

Goodie!
(*Scrambles down*)

FAY

Really, Mr. Cooley, as the father of eleven natural children, you should know that child will catch her death of cold sitting in all that damp. Baby Joan—home and change those panties.

BABY JOAN

I gotta sell blessings.

FAY

After you change.

BABY JOAN

(*Threatening*)

I'll go into a trance.

FAY

After you change. Scoot!
(BABY JOAN *stalks off as* SCHUB *enters opposite*)

COOLEY

(*To* FAY)

Forty-nine tickets for your forty-nine Cookies reckons up to—

SCHUB

Treasurer, a word with you? Magruder, hold the line. A brief moment, my dear Head-nursie. (*Takes* COOLEY *to one side*) Cooley, you are stupid beyond the dreams of man. Don't you know those loonies from Dr. Detmold's sanitarium will be just as looney *after* they take the waters as they were before?

COOLEY

So what, Brother? Forty-nine full-rate tickets—

SCHUB

If forty-nine people partake of that miracle in one fell group, and nothing happens, don't you think someone is going to be suspicious of something?

COOLEY

Sister Apple, we're fresh out of tickets.

FAY

(*Advancing on them*)

No, Mr. Cooley.

SCHUB

My dear up-dated Nightingale—

FAY

No, Mr. Schub.

SCHUB

Now, Nursie, why do you want your Cookies to take the waters? They're well-fed, well-housed, well-clothed; they're happy—

FAY

Are they? Oh, they smile according to their schedules, but they're in limbo while they're in The Jar. I want them out and free to be happy or unhappy any way *they* want.

SCHUB

And do you think our miracle can do anything for them?

FAY

If it can do anything for anyone.

SCHUB

My dear devoted Whitenurse, you're a woman of science: age of reason, ego and id, order and control. Do you honestly believe in people being healed by mere faith?

FAY

Faith in dirty water from a slimy old rock? No.

SCHUB

Aha! Exposed!

FAY

Who?

SCHUB

You, you anarchist! You can't believe in anything that can't be proved in your laboratory of a head! All miracles are fake to you, Nurse Apple. You're in love with science, Nurse Apple; you sleep with discipline, Nurse Apple; you have a core of stone, Nurse Apple. Let these happy hopeful Pilgrims be lost and miserable, again, eh? Let this boom town be a ghost town again, eh? Let those forty-nine loonies—

FAY

NOT—THAT—WORD! (*Fast vamp under*) Nor any word like it! Cookies, Schub, that's what my charges are: Cookies from The Cookie Jar. Patients from Dr. Detmold's Asylum for the Socially Pressured. Quarantined out of fear their disease may be contagious, they are people who made other people nervous by leading individual lives. They suffer from contact with groups and systems, I won't specify who or what. But if the shoe fits, boys, you put your foot in it. NOW—POINT —ONE! (*Music up a key and faster*) I *am* in love with reason and against any balderdash superstition that holds up progress, and those dripping waters of yours not only hold it up, they flood and drown it. My name is Apple, A-Double P-L-E, a fruit well-mentioned in the Bible, that best seller of

many miracles. I cite the Ten Commandments and the Burn-
ing Bush, to mention only two. Or eleven—depending on
your arithmetic. Mine makes them add up to zero because I
personally am for the miracles of man such as the wheel, the
alphabet and The Pyramids of Egypt! NOW—
POINT—TWO! (*Music, as above*) If that exposed sewer sys-
tem *is* a miracle, I freely admit I will take a running jump in
the origin of that water. What is more, if it can make any of
those lazy pilgrims—yes they're lazy, trying to get a new life
quick—if it can make any of them permanently happy, I will
take three running jumps and only come up twice. But I will
bet you that the same thing will happen that happens every-
time you sell people a myth. Those water works will turn out
not to be a miracle and those pilgrims are going to end up
pounding on our doors! Well, we have no room, Schub. Every
bed is full and they are sleeping in shifts! There is no more
room in The Jar! NOW—POINT—THREE!!! (*Music, as
above*) If these are my beliefs, and they are, why do I want
my Cookies to take your waters? I'll tell you why. Because my
Cookies are people, Schub, they are human beings and they
are to be treated as such and have the same rights as everyone
else! You let them sit in your movies, Schub, although you
make them sit in a segregated section. You let them charge in
your stores, Cooley—although you make them pay on the
ninth and not the tenth of the month. So you both can bloody
well let them dip into that leaking drain pipe. If you don't
I'm not saying I'll go to the police because I am no fool. Nor
will I go to the Mayoress because she is. But this is a free
town in a free county in a free state in a free country and I
am a free woman with a free mouth and if you say No to my
Cookies, I will open up that mouth and talk and I am telling
you here and now that when I talk, I talk *LONG-AND-
LOUD!!!*
    (*Music finishes with a crash*)

COOLEY

Mercy!

SCHUB

Apple, you will be rotting in the cellar at the bottom of the
jail unless your people are conducted back—(*He stops. He,*
FAY *and* COOLEY *have been on one side. On the other, the*
line of COOKIES *has unobtrusively blended right into the line*
of PILGRIMS) Where are they?

FAY

There.

SCHUB

Where?

FAY

There.

SCHUB

But *where* are they there?
          (*Slowly, she smiles sweetly at him. He forces a smile*
          back)

MAGRUDER

All right, now. Who's who?

SCHUB

Shut up. (*To the line*) My dear citizens, will all those who
are pilgrims kindly take one short step forward?
          (*They all do*)

FAY

Dear friends, will all those who believe in miracles, clap your hands!

(*Everybody does*)

COOLEY

Hear me, Brethren. Everybody who bought one of these red tickets to the miracle, raise it up—high! (*Slowly, one by one, each person on line raises a red ticket*) She stole 'em!

SCHUB

Are you going to say which is which?

FAY

Are you going to let everyone take that water?

SCHUB

No!

FAY

Then No to you!

SCHUB

Then to jail with you!

FAY

You can put me in jail—when you catch me!

(*She starts to run. Instantly, some of the* COOKIES *move to block* SCHUB, COOLEY *and* MAGRUDER. PILGRIMS *on the line move in confusion. This movement is very quick, for all the lights go out except a spot on*

FAY; *everyone else freezes in an attitude of chasing or protecting her. The angry music from her earlier speech begins underneath and she sings)*

FAY

Those smug little men with their smug little schemes,
They forgot one thing:
The play isn't over by a long shot yet!
There are heroes in the world,
Princes and heroes in the world,
And one of them will save me.
Wait and see!
Wait and see!

There won't be trumpets or bolts of fire
To say he's coming.
No Roman candles, no angels' choir,
No sound of distant drumming.
   He may not be the cavalier,
   Tall and graceful, fair and strong.
   Doesn't matter,
   Just as long as he comes along!
But not with trumpets or lightning flashing
Or shining armor.
He may be daring, he may be dashing,
Or maybe he's a farmer.
I can wait—what's another day?
He has lots of hills to climb.
And a hero
Doesn't come till the nick of time!
Don't look for trumpets or whistles tooting
To guarantee him!
There won't be trumpets, but sure as shooting
I'll know him when I see him!

Don't know when, don't know where,
And I can't even say that I care!
All I know is, the minute I turn and he's suddenly there
I won't need trumpets!
There are no trumpets!
Who needs trumpets?
> (*After the song, the lights return. The freeze is broken by* FAY *who breaks through the crowd and dashes behind the rock as:*)

SCHUB

Don't let her get away! Police!

MAGRUDER

Police!

SCHUB

Idiot! (*To* COOLEY) Go to The Cookie Jar and get Dr. Detmold. (*To* MAGRUDER) You fool, arrest her at once!

MAGRUDER

> (*Grabs the sexy teen-ager he is standing next to*)
Thank you.

SCHUB

Not her, you sex fiend! The nurse! The nurse!

MAGRUDER

Oh, the nurse, the nurse!
> (*Runs off*)

SCHUB

(To the crowd)

My dear idiots, excuse my friends. I mean—my dear friends, I must ask you to refrain, for the moment, from taking the waters. *(But the crowd now re-forms its line)* While it is true that it is a miracle—

> *(Suddenly, there is a great clap of thunder, several flashes of lightning, trumpet calls—which nobody notices—and on walks a very personable man, dressed casually and carrying a small, oblong case:* J. BOWDEN HAPGOOD. *Behind him is a nondescript man carrying a large suitcase)*

HAPGOOD

Excuse me, but could you direct me to The Cookie Jar?

SCHUB

What for?! There's nobody there, they're all here.

HAPGOOD

Where?

SCHUB

There.

HAPGOOD

(Smiling)

They don't look it.

SCHUB

Of course they don't look it because all of them aren't!

HAPGOOD

Well, which ones are?

SCHUB

You're asking me?!

HAPGOOD

Not really.

SCHUB

You can't tell by looking anyway! Do I look it?

HAPGOOD

Actually, no.

SCHUB

There you are!

HAPGOOD

Then why aren't you there?

SCHUB

Why should I be?

HAPGOOD

Oh, you mean they allow you to wander around.

SCHUB

I mean I'm here because I belong here! I'm in charge!

HAPGOOD

You can't be Dr. Detmold!

SCHUB

Of course I'm not Dr. Detmold! He isn't here; he's at The Cookie Jar.

HAPGOOD

Ah! And—which way *is* The Cookie Jar?

SCHUB.

That way.

HAPGOOD

(*To his companion*)
No wonder it takes so long to get anywhere. (*To* SCHUB, *indicating the waters*) By the way, what is that?

SCHUB

It's perfectly obvious what that is. That's a miracle, that's what that is.

HAPGOOD

Thank you. See you at The Cookie Jar.
(*And he exits with his companion*)

SCHUB

Where was I? Where *am* I?

CORA

(*Off—singing* a capella)
Schub! Comptroller Schub!

SCHUB

O, Father in Heaven—(*As* CORA *enters*) My dear Madam Mayor, I regret—

CORA

(A capella)
I don't want to hear it! Don't tell me! (*Speaks, in disgust*) You blew it. Well, I absolutely refuse to be hated again. Where's Dr. Detmold?
(*On this, a fussy, businesslike-looking man with gray hair enters:* DR. DETMOLD)

DETMOLD

In a temper (*He laughs*) Schub, I am in the midst of writing an extremely revolutionary paper for our *Quarterly Monthly*—

SCHUB

Who in that line is a patient of yours?

DETMOLD

You interrupt me and progress to ask that? My new assistant will help you. He is younger but less eminent.
(*He laughs again*)

CORA

Ah! And where is he?

DETMOLD

He knows, I don't.

SCHUB

Doctor, it is a simple matter for you to point out who on that line you know and who—

DETMOLD

It is *not* simple! Psychiatrists do not fraternize with patients so how can we recognize them? We see them only during the analytic hour—when they are lying down. I can do nothing.
(*He starts to go*)

CORA

Detmold. We are not amused.

DETMOLD

(*Cringing*)
Your Honor, we doctors are underworked and overpaid. Surely you can wait for my new assistant? He was due several patients ago but I'm—
(*Behind them the drunken* NURSE *enters, cozily hanging on* HAPGOOD'S *arm. He carries both cases now*)

NURSE

Ahoy, Doctor . . .

DETMOLD

(*Joyously*)
Doctor!
(*He extends his hand*)

HAPGOOD

(*Shaking hands*)
Doctor.

DETMOLD

Detmold, L. Sidney.

HAPGOOD

Hapgood, J. Bowden.

DETMOLD

Of course! I may be terrible on faces but I never remember
a name. Mayor Schub, Comptroller Hoover Hooper, my new
assistant, Dr. Jay.

HAPGOOD *and* SCHUB

(*Simultaneously*)

Doctor—

CORA

He's Schub, you're Hapgood and I'm delighted.

DETMOLD

So am I. Doctor, take care of these good people. Nurse,
take the doctor's luggage to the hotel.

HAPGOOD

Just a minute—

DETMOLD

If you need help, bring your dreams to The Cookie Jar and
my new assistant will take care of you.
     (*He laughs and goes*)

CORA
(*Leering*)

Hello . . .

HAPGOOD

Hello . . .

CORA

So *you* are going to take care of *me*.

SCHUB

First he's going to take care of us. Now Doctor, here's our problem in a nutshell.

CORA

Oh Schub! Ha ha ha ha!

HAPGOOD

(*Aside to* SCHUB)

She's the Mayor . . . ?

SCHUB

Yes: *I'm* the Comptroller. You know about our miracle.

HAPGOOD

Oh yes.
(*He winks at* CORA)

SCHUB

Why are you winking?

HAPGOOD

I wasn't winking. It's just a tic.

SCHUB

It *is* a miracle.

HAPGOOD

Oh yes, so you said. And so I've heard. I think I heard everything from that alcoholic nurse.

SCHUB

Then you realize that we must know immediately which of the people on that line are bona fide pilgrims, entitled to take our miracle waters, and which are—

HAPGOOD

Cookies.

SCHUB

Yes.

HAPGOOD

(Shakes his hand, then CORA's)
Good-bye. Good-bye.

CORA

Doctor!

HAPGOOD

(Leaving)
You've got the wrong man.

SCHUB

Stop him!
>   (COOLEY *and a deputy, holding guns, appear and*
>   *block* HAPGOOD. *He turns and* MAGRUDER *runs on*
>   *from the other side, a* DEPUTY *behind him*)

MAGRUDER

Your Honor, we can't find a trace of Nurse Apple! She's completely disappeared!

SCHUB

Set up road blocks—get out the police dogs—

CORA

You can borrow mine.

SCHUB

But—Hunt—Her—Down! (DEPUTY *runs off*) Now Doctor, you're an eminent psychiatrist, aren't you?

HAPGOOD

No.

SCHUB

I loathe modesty.

HAPGOOD

Even if I were Freud, I've just arrived here! How can I tell you like that who's a pilgrim and who's a Cookie?

CORA

I'm sure you can.

HAPGOOD

Your Honor—

CORA

Dear Doctor—

HAPGOOD

Dear Mayor—

CORA

—ess.

HAPGOOD

That—is obvious.

CORA

You know, you're divine!

HAPGOOD

Shall we dance?

CORA

Your place or mine?

HAPGOOD

Here and now!
(*Tosses his hat away, the orchestra strikes up and they dance*)

SCHUB

What the hell is this?

HAPGOOD

I have to think and I think best on my feet.

SCHUB

Dancing??

HAPGOOD

Well, usually, I walk. But when I don't want to get anywhere, I dance.

SCHUB

My dear Doctor, it is very urgent we all get somewhere—*fast.*

(*Yanks him out of the dance, ending the music*)

HAPGOOD

. . . Are you cutting in, Schub? Because I don't like—

CORA

Dr. Hapgood, it's *Comptroller* Schub. He is *my* comptroller; this is *my* town; that is *my* miracle. Dr. Detmold, of course, is *your* superior, but he is just another of *my* tax payers. And like all tax payers he is, of course, behind in his taxes. Which means that he—and therefore, *you*—are at *my* disposal. Like garbage. Which means that oh my God, when I look into your eyes, I wish I'd lost that election.

HAPGOOD

I see your problem. And mine. Yesterday mine would have upset me. But today—I'll have fun solving it!

SCHUB

Fun? I'm not following.

HAPGOOD

No, you're leading. That is you were. But now I shall. May I have this dance?

SCHUB

Sir?!

HAPGOOD

With Her Honor. I really do think best on my feet, Comptroller. And I must think out a quick way to discover who is who, what is what and make everybody—

SCHUB

Yes . . . ?

HAPGOOD

Happy. (*Holding out his arms*) Mayor?

CORA

You may.
      (*A deep curtsey*)

SCHUB

Then on with the dance! (*Orchestra blast, and they're off!! Motioning them toward the line*) No, no. They're over here.

CORA

(*To* HAPGOOD)
Oh, I could think all night!

SCHUB

We haven't got all night. Can't you pick up the tempo?

HAPGOOD

No: Give me a fanfare!

CORA

While we're dancing?

HAPGOOD

To announce I'm going to sing to you.

CORA

Brilliant! Dear man, sing it all! (*A fanfare*) But how are you going to separate them?

HAPGOOD

I'm going to examine them according to the principles of logic.

CORA

Logic?

HAPGOOD

It's quick and easy.

(*Sings*)

Grass is green,
Sky is blue,
False is false and
True is true.
Who is who?

You are you,
I'm me!
Simple? Simple? Simple?
Simple as ABC.
Simple as one-two-three!

SCHUB

But who on that line is what?

HAPGOOD

(*Sings*)

One is one,
Two is two,
Who is what and
Which is who?
No one's always what they seem to be.

CORA

(*A crack at* SCHUB)

That's certainly true.

HAPGOOD

(*Sings*)

Simple? Simple? Simple?
Simple as A-B-C.
Simple as one-two three.

(*Music continues under. He speaks to a young man on the line*)

For example—you, sir, with the manly good looks. Would you come forward please, Mr. Hapgood?

SCHUB

I thought you were Hapgood.

HAPGOOD

Calling the patient by my name, he identifies with me immediately, we have an instant transference and thereby save five years of psychoanalysis.

CORA

Brilliant! What happens if I call you Hoover Hooper?

HAPGOOD

Shall we dance? No, we have. Now then, Mr. Hapgood—

GEORGE (The YOUNG MAN)

Call me Happy, Sir. Or George.

HAPGOOD

All right, Georgie.

GEORGE

Thank you, George.

HAPGOOD

Thank *you*. Now when we were a child, that is, when you were a child, a boy—you *were* a boy?

GEORGE

I was a manly little fellow, sir.

HAPGOOD

Then I'm sure there was a saying you learned that you have used ever since to govern your life. A motto, a watchcry.

GEORGE

A watchcry. Yes, sir. (*He sings*) "I am the master of my fate and the captain of my soul."

HAPGOOD

Good, Hapgood! Now then: (*Following is spoken rhythmically to orchestral vamp*) Married?

GEORGE

Yes, sir.

HAPGOOD

Two children?

GEORGE

Yes, sir.

HAPGOOD

Two TV sets?

GEORGE

Yes, sir.

HAPGOOD

Two martinis?

GEORGE

Yes, sir.

HAPGOOD

Bank on Friday?

GEORGE

Yes, sir.

HAPGOOD

Golf on Saturday?

GEORGE

Yes, sir.

HAPGOOD

Church on Sunday?

GEORGE

Yes, sir.

HAPGOOD

Do you vote?

GEORGE

Only for the man who wins.
Only for the man who wins.
Only for the man who—

HAPGOOD

(*Holds up his hand*)
All right. Headaches?

GEORGE

No, sir.

HAPGOOD

Backaches?

GEORGE

No, sir.

HAPGOOD

Heartaches?

GEORGE

No, sir.

HAPGOOD

Thank you, Hapgood. (*Music out*) Group A. Over there, please.

SCHUB

(*To* CORA)

What's Group A?

CORA

Obviously mad as a hatter.

SCHUB

Magruder! Place that Cookie under arrest.

HAPGOOD

Just a moment. (*To* GEORGE) George—do you ever wonder whether you're real?

GEORGE

No, sir. I know I'm not.

HAPGOOD

Group One. Over *there*, please.
  (*As* GEORGE *crosses to the opposite side, the music
  returns and* HAPGOOD *sings*)
Grass is green,
Sky is blue
Safe is sane and
Tried is true.
You be you and me to some degree.
Simple? Simple? Simple as A-B-C,
Simple as one-two-three.

CORA

Well, is he safe or sane, Doctor? Darling.

SCHUB

Safe *is* sane.

HAPGOOD

Not always.
  (*He sings*)
The opposite of safe is out.
The opposite of out is in.
So anyone who's safe is "in."

GEORGE

  (*He sings*)
That I've always been!

CORA

Shh!
(*She sings, joined by* SCHUB, COOLEY *and* MAGRUDER)
The opposite of safe is out.
The opposite of out is in.
So anyone who's safe is "in."

HAPGOOD

Right!
        (*He sings*)
That's how groups begin!

CORA, *et al*

When you're in, you win!

HAPGOOD

Simple? Simple? Simple?
Simple as A-B-C.

CORA, *et al*

Simple? Simple? Simple?

HAPGOOD

Simple as do you do like me?

CORA

(*Cooing*)
I do indeed like you. The question is—

SCHUB

(*Overriding impatiently*)
The question is—(*To a* MAN *who has been sneaking over to* GEORGE) Just a moment there—

MAN

(*Sings*)
"I am the master of my fate and the captain of my soul."
(*He speaks*) But my name isn't George, Doctor.

HAPGOOD

What is it?

MAN

Hapgood.

HAPGOOD

Group A. Over there, please.
(CORA *and* SCHUB *look at each other*)

SCHUB

What *is* this?

CORA

I don't know, but it's brilliant.

SCHUB

But which group is what?

HAPGOOD

It's very simple.
    (*He sings*)
Grass is green,
Sky is blue,
A is one group,
One is too,
One is One or one is A, you see . . .

CORA

(*Nodding brightly, sings*)
Grass is green,
Sky is blue,
One is one and
A is two.

SCHUB

(*Sings*)

No, A is one and
One is, too.

SIMULTANEOUSLY

CORA	COOLEY	MAGRUDER	SCHUB
No, one and one			
Is always two	No, One is green,		
To me!	A is blue.	No, A is green,	
	One can be	One is blue!	No, One is One,
I don't agree!	In A, you see.	A is "out" and	A is one group,
A is you and	A is crazy!	One is "in"!	Too.
Me!	Maybe.	I agree.	See?

(*They are interrupted by a* WOMAN *who sings in a strong contralto and comes forward at* HAPGOOD'S *beckoning*)

WOMAN

(Very loud)

Aaaaaaaaaaaaaaaaa—

(She is joined by a MAN; she is in a very feminine dress, he in a threadbare suit; she keeps dropping a handkerchief for him to pick up, he has a tin cup she keeps dropping coins into)

MAN and WOMAN

(Singing, a nervous accompaniment underneath)
A woman's place is in the home,
A woman's place is in the house.
And home is where you hang your hat,
And that is where you hang your spouse.

HAPGOOD

(Speaks, as music contines)
Dear Mr. and Mrs. Hapgood.

JUNE (The WOMAN)

Oh, we're not married, Doctor. He's June and I'm John. I mean she's John and he's June.

JOHN

June and John are engaged.

JUNE

John's my secretary.

JOHN

June used to be my secretary but his corporation went bust.

JUNE

And her syndicate took over.

HAPGOOD

Well, it would all be in the family if you got married.

JOHN

But John can't support June.

JUNE

Every cent John makes goes to pay for June's dinners.

HAPGOOD

Why doesn't June give John a raise?

JUNE

He's not worth it.

HAPGOOD

I see. And neither of you wants John to stay home and do the housekeeping because—

HAPGOOD, JUNE, JOHN

(Sing)
A woman's place is in the home,
A woman's place is on the shelf.
And home is where he hangs her hat,
And that is where she hangs himself.

CORA *and* SCHUB

(*Expectantly*)

Group—
(*Music stops*)

HAPGOOD

(*To* JUNE)

A.

SCHUB

Magruder!

HAPGOOD

(*To* JOHN)

One.

(*Music resumes.* HAPGOOD *steers him away from* JUNE *as* ANOTHER COUPLE *and* JUNE *and* JOHN *again sing "A Woman's Place is in the Home" while* GEORGE *and the* SNEAKING MAN *sing "I am the Master of my Fate."* HAPGOOD *directs the* WOMAN *to One and the* MAN *to A. Everybody stares; there is more singing of watchcries, during which* HAPGOOD *splits the singers into one or the other of the Groups and during which* PEOPLE *from each Group—or the line—cross to the other side*)

PEOPLE

(*Sing, simultaneously*)

"A woman's place is in the home, a woman's place is in the house."

"I am the master of my fate and the captain of my soul."

"If at first you don't succeed, try, try again."

"Beauty is only skin deep."

SCHUB

Stop the music! (*It does*) A man crossed over.

HAPGOOD

That was a woman.

SCHUB

Oh.

CORA

(*Pushing* SCHUB)
Group One. (*Music re-enters under*) *Ha ha ha ha ha!*

SCHUB

Now wait! Are they *all* Cookies? If you could produce
someone who is sane, present company excluded, of course—
(*A Negro steps forward as* HAPGOOD *beckons*)

HAPGOOD

Ah—good lad, Hapgood. Watchcry!

MARTIN (The NEGRO)

(*Sings*)
You can't judge a book by its cover.
You can't judge a book by its cover.
You can't judge a book
By how literate it look,
No, you can't judge a book by its cubber.
(*Music continues under*)

HAPGOOD

Occupation?

MARTIN

Going to schools, riding in buses, eating in restaurants.

HAPGOOD

Isn't that line of work getting rather easy?

MARTIN

Not for me. I'm Jewish . . . Group A, would you say?

HAPGOOD

Group One's more fun.

MARTIN

Crazy.

CORA

Group A . . .

SCHUB

Group One . . .

CORA

It's maddening!

SCHUB

What's the difference between them?

HAPGOOD

It's obvious:
    (Sings)
The opposite of dark is bright,

The opposite of bright is dumb.
So anything that's dark is dumb—

MARTIN

But they sure can hum.
>   (HAPGOOD *and* TWO MEN—*one each from Groups A
>   and One—hum a close-harmony counterpoint to*
>   MARTIN)

The opposite of dark is bright,
The opposite of bright is dumb.

HAPGOOD, MARTIN, TWO MEN

So anything that's dark is dumb.

HAPGOOD, TWO MEN

That's the rule of thumb.

MARTIN

Depends where you're from.

HAPGOOD

>   (*As* MARTIN *shuffles over to One, Uncle Tom style*)

Simple? Simple? Simple?
Simple as A-B-C.
Simple as NAACP!
>   (*Music continues under*)

MAN

I get the point, Comptroller Hapgood.

SCHUB

Oh, shut up and get in Group A.

CORA

Who's that?

SCHUB

My brother-in-law.

CORA

But he's not a Pilgrim . . . and he's not a Cookie—Hapgood . . .

HAPGOOD

(*Grins and starts to sing; the music takes on a slightly sinister tone; slowly the line and the rock begin to move upstage*)
Who is what?
Which is who?
That is that and
How are you?
I feel fine, what else is new?

CORA

(*During the above*)
What was he doing on the line?

SCHUB

Oh . . . every fool wants a miracle. Hapgood—

CORA

Who *is* on that line? . . .

SCHUB

Doctor, you are not doing what we want you to!

CORA

You're right! Look here, Hapgood—(*But he holds out his arms to her*)—darling—
> (*They dance as she sings; the music becomes a gay waltz*)

Grass is green,
Sky is blue,
I'd join any Group with you.
Schub's a boob and you belong to me!
Simple? Simple? Simple?
Simple as one-two-three, one-two-three, one-two-three . . .
> (*Some of the* PEOPLE *on the line pick up the refrain with delight. A few crowd around* HAPGOOD)

PEOPLE

Doctor, what Group am I in? Where do I belong? Where am I? Tell me where I am? Where am I?!
> (HAPGOOD *directs them to one or the other of the Groups until there is no one left on the line*)

SCHUB

> (*Pushing through*)

Get back! Your Honor! Cora! He's taking over! They're turning to *him*! Stop it! (*Music suddenly becomes low and sinister; little scenery is left; upstage area darkens*) Doctor— Group A: Cookies? Or Group One: Cookies? The truth now —Which—is—what?

HAPGOOD

> (*Suddenly, to Group A*)

Watchcry!

GROUP A

(Singing simultaneously)
"I am the master of my fate and—"
"A woman's place is in the—"
"If at first you don't succeed—"
      (HAPGOOD *cuts them off suddenly and sharply*)

HAPGOOD

Rub your stomachs!
      (They do)
Goo-ood. Goo-ood.
      (To Group One)
Watchcry!

GROUP ONE

(Singing simultaneously)
"I am the master of my fate and—"
"A woman's place is in the—"
"Beauty is only skin—"
      (HAPGOOD *cuts them off*)

HAPGOOD

Pat your heads. *(They do)* Hello. Hello . . . Goo-ood . . .
Hello. Hello . . . Reverse! Good. Hello. Hello. That's goo-
ood, goo-ood, goo-ood, goo-ood, Comptroller.

SCHUB

(Who has started doing it)
Dammit!

CORA

I adore games!

HAPGOOD

Watchcry!

CORA

Hello.

SCHUB

He's boring from within!

HAPGOOD

(*To* SCHUB)

Watchcry!

SCHUB

Communist!

HAPGOOD

You would say that.
      (*Sings*)
The opposite of Left is right,
The opposite of right is wrong,
So anyone who's Left is wrong, right?

CROWD

Goo-ood! Goo-ood!

HAPGOOD

Hello!

CROWD

Hello!

HAPGOOD

(*Sings, to* SCHUB)
Simple? Simple? Simple?
Simple as you tell me!
Simple as one-two-three
Cheers for the Red, White and Blue . . .
(*To* MAGRUDER, *as he instinctively straightens to at-
tention*)
Watchcry!

MAGRUDER

Look here: I'm the Chief of—

HAPGOOD

Watchcry!
(*The music, still sinister, becomes martial*)

MAGRUDER

(*Sings*)
"Ours not to reason why, ours but to do or die."
(*Speaks*)
Sergeant Magruder reporting, sir.

HAPGOOD

Occupation?

MAGRUDER

Fighting the enemy.

HAPGOOD

What enemy?

MAGRUDER

What year?

HAPGOOD

Yesterday:

MAGRUDER
(*Angrily*)

The Germans: *Heil!*

HAPGOOD

The day before:

MAGRUDER
(*Angrily*)

The Germans: *Heil!*

HAPGOOD

Today:

MAGRUDER
(*Beaming*)

The Germans: Hail!

HAPGOOD

Tomorrow:

MAGRUDER
(*Beaming*)

Hail!
(*Angrily*)

Heil!
    (*Puzzled*)
Hail? . . . *Heil?* . . . Hail?

HAPGOOD

Group A.

MAGRUDER

Heil?

HAPGOOD

Group One.

MAGRUDER

Hail?
    (*He is marching back and forth*)

COOLEY

You're just making him *seem* crazy, but he's twisted. I mean—he's been twisted.

HAPGOOD
    (*Sings*)

Grass is blue,
Sky is green,
Change of time is change of scene.
What you meant is what you mean!
    (*Wheeling on* COOLEY)
Watchcry!

COOLEY

Hallelujah! Now listen, Brother—

HAPGOOD

Occupation:

COOLEY

Preacher—er, Treasurer.

HAPGOOD

Oh, you *were* a preacher, Hapgood.

COOLEY

I'm a treasurer, Cooley—I mean—

HAPGOOD

They threw you out of your pulpit—

COOLEY

(*To* SCHUB)

Brother!

HAPGOOD

Because you were crazy!

COOLEY

Because I believed!

HAPGOOD

In being treasurer.

COOLEY

In God, and they only believed in religion.

HAPGOOD

And *that* made you crazy, Hapgood.

COOLEY

I am *not* crazy, Cooley!

HAPGOOD

No, you're Crazy Hapgood.

COOLEY

I am not Cooley, I mean I am not crazy, I'm Hapgood!

HAPGOOD

Are you sure?

COOLEY

I am completely Schub!

SCHUB

He's crazy!

HAPGOOD

Thank you.
    (*To* COOLEY)
Group A.
    (*To Group One*)
Watchcry!
    (*They respond automatically; immediately, to Group
    A*)
Watchcry!
    (*They respond; to* SCHUB)
Watchcry!

SCHUB

I don't have one, Cooley!

HAPGOOD

Ah ha!
(*The chanting stops; the music drops to a single spaced beat under*)

SCHUB

Hapgood, we are going to end all this right here and now, my dear Treasurer, I mean Doctor, dammit! Right now: which group is—

HAPGOOD

Two questions.

SCHUB

One answer.

HAPGOOD

Just two little questions, Schub, and you'll *know* which group is what. (*Percussion starts low, under*) Where does most of your money go?

SCHUB

I hardly—

HAPGOOD

Where does most of your money go, Hapgood?

SCHUB

In taxes.

HAPGOOD

(*Motioning to Group One to start gesture*)
Goo-od. (*To* SCHUB) What do you think of someone who makes a product and doesn't use it?

SCHUB

He's crazy.

HAPGOOD

(*To second Group*)
Hello, hello. (*They continue as he turns to* SCHUB) Most of your money goes to the government in taxes. What does the government do with most of the money? Makes bombs. (*To the Groups*) Reverse! Goo-od. Hello, hello. (*To* SCHUB) But you say to make a product and not to use it is crazy. Isn't that what you said, Comptroller Cooley? And doesn't that make you crazy for letting them waste your money, Treasurer Schub? (*To the Groups*) Reverse! (*To* SCHUB) But perhaps the government is making bombs because it means to use the product. Which means everyone will be killed, Hapgood. Including you, Schub. (*To the Groups*) Both together now! (*They do both gestures. To* SCHUB) Which means you are paying most of your money to have yourself killed. Which means, my dear Doctor Comptroller Mayor Schub, you are the maddest of all! Watchcry!

SCHUB

HELP!!
(*He runs off*)

HAPGOOD

WATCHCRY!

CORA

BRILLIANT!!

HAPGOOD

WATCHCRY!
(*And now everybody on stage begins a chant, led by a wild, cheering, jeering* HAPGOOD. CORA, *at first amused, picks up the chant but then gets more and more frightened as the two Groups form a circle, at* HAPGOOD'S *direction, which gets smaller until it closes in on her completely*)

GROUPS

Grass is green.
Sky is blue.
The opposite of left is right.
The opposite of right is wrong.
Simple? Simple? Simple?
Simple as A-B-three,
Simple as one-two-C,
As grass is green
As sky is blue;
As simple as the opposite of left is right
Is wrong Is right Is A Is One
Is A Is One Hello! Hello! Goo-od! Goo-od!
A is One! One is A!
Grass is who is opposite of what is green is safe is opposite
Of dark is opposite of simple which is
Watchcry! Watchcry! Watchcry! Watchcry!
(*The Groups have now crushed* CORA *in their center;* HAPGOOD *is sitting at the footlights. There is a loud furious drum break as* CORA *is tossed in the air like a broken puppet. The light goes almost black except for*

*a weird glow from the footlights. The two Groups run
down to the footlights and, in a straight line right
across the stage, chant fast and shrill, with mounting
intensity)*

Who is what? Which is who?

Who is what? Which is who?

Who is what? Which is WHO is WHO?

(Silence and blackout except for a light on HAPGOOD.
*He looks at the audience with a smile and says,
quietly)*

HAPGOOD

You are all mad.

*(There is a burst of gay, wild circus music. A row of
lights resembling the balcony rail of a theatre has
been lowered and it now begins to burn brighter and
brighter with pink, blue, yellow lights, flooding the
theatre audience. At the same time, the real balcony
rail lights in the theatre are coming on and lighting
up the stage. And there we see the company sitting in
theatre seats and laughing and applauding louder and
louder as*

The Curtain Falls

ACT TWO

The theatre seats are now in the town square. A center aisle separates them so that they look like bleachers. One side has pennants and placards reading Group A; the other side has similar signs reading Group One. As the two Groups sing the following march, HAPGOOD *is carried on by two members of each Group on* CORA's *litter and is cheered and besieged for autographs.*

GROUP A

Hooray for A, the Group that's well-adjusted,
Everyone can be trusted in Group A.

GROUP ONE

Have fun with One, the Group that's not neurotic,
Everyone's patriotic in Group One.

BOTH

Dignity, integrity and so on,
We haven't much to go on,
Still we go on.
We've a platform strong enough to grow on:

GROUP A

Whenever they cheer, we're incensed!

GROUP ONE

Whatever they're for, we're against!
    (HAPGOOD *enters*)

GROUP A

Hooray for Hapgood,
Hapgood can be trusted,
Friend of the well-adjusted in Group A!

GROUP ONE

Hooray for Hapgood
Hapgood's patriotic,
Friend of the un-neurotic in Group One!

BOTH

Hapgood has no answers or suggestions,
Only a lot of questions—
We like questions.
What's the use of answers or suggestions?
As long as we're told where to go,
There isn't a thing we need to know!

> (*The march never really ends; it fades off as both Groups leave their seats and march out after* HAPGOOD, *aloft on his litter. As the last marchers clear, a flamboyantly sexy-looking creature is revealed sitting in one of the theatre seats, glancing through a program. She wears an extravagant red coat trimmed with feathers, dark glasses and a red wig.* SCHUB *enters, sees her, preens and takes a seat near her. He doesn't recognize her but we do. Or we will. It is* FAY APPLE *who speaks with one of the thickest French accents in captivity*)

FAY

Bon—jour.

SCHUB

A very *bonjour* to you, my dear, dear Madame.

FAY

Mademoiselle—unfortunately. (*She* and SCHUB *get out of the seats which slide off, revealing a small red traveling case*) I am—(*A hot chord blasts from the orchestra*) Colette—(*Chord*)—Antoinette—(*Chord*)—Alouette—(*Chord*)—Mistinguette—(*Chord*)—Alfabette—(*Chord*)—de—la—Val—lere: Ze lady from Lourdes!

> (*Instantly, music;* CORA'S *four* BOYS *pop out and with* FAY *sing* à la "*The Lady in Red*")

FAY *and* BOYS

Ze Lady from Lourdes,
Ze boys are all crazy bout ze
Lady from Lourdes!
Ooh, la la!

> (*The* BOYS *exit*)

SCHUB

Lourdes is in France, I gather.

FAY

Oui, monsieur.

SCHUB

You must be very weary after your journey. Why don't we have an *apéritif* this evening? My place, seven-thirty. Better make that six-thirty. Your place. Or mine. It makes no difference. Your place at six. Sharp.

FAY

I have ze work to do first, *monsieur*.

SCHUB

Work?

FAY

Certainement. I am from Lourdes.

SCHUB

So you sang . . . What are you looking at?
(*Across the stage,* HAPGOOD *appears on the balcony of
the Hotel Superbe with cigar and champagne.*
SCHUB's *back is to him, but he and* FAY *are facing
each other*)

FAY

Zat *docteur*. He is ze most important man in town, no?

SCHUB

No. I'm the most important man in town—next to the
Mayor-ess.

FAY

Zen you are ze man to 'elp me! *Monsieur* knows that which
Lourdes she is famous for, no?

SCHUB

L'amour?

FAY

No, no, *monsieur*.

SCHUB

La sexe?

FAY

Ah, you make ze funny of me. (*She and* HAPGOOD *leer at each other. She beckons to him; he leans closer; she beckons again and the scenery obliges: the whole balcony moves to her. During this, she continues to* SCHUB) Ze whole world, she know that which Lourdes she is famous for, is—*la miracle! Et moi*—me—I am sent 'ere to investigate your miracle.

SCHUB

To investigate—my—miracle.

FAY

Oui. Since Lourdes, she is ze mama of all ze miracles, so we ladies from Lourdes, we go all over ze globe to see if ze new little baby miracles are 'ow you say—legitimate.

SCHUB

If you'll excuse me, dear *mademoiselle*, I think I must go home and faint.
(*He exits*)

FAY

Au'voir, monsieur.
(*She tosses her dark glasses away, and she and* HAPGOOD *smile at each other. During their conversation subtitles are flashed on, indicated here by parentheses. Everything is spoken as though they were in an old French sex film*)

FAY

Il est fou. (He's mad.)

HAPGOOD

Tout le monde est fou, sauf vous et moi. (The whole world's mad—except you and me.)

FAY

Et bien—bonjour! (Well, then—hello!)

HAPGOOD

Comment ça va? (How are you?)

FAY

Bien. Êtes-vous marié? (Well. Are you married?)

HAPGOOD

Quatre fois. (Four times.)

FAY

Au'voir. (Good-bye.)
      (*She starts to go*)

HAPGOOD

Mais, je suis divorcé! (But I'm divorced!)

FAY

Combien de fois? (How many times?)

HAPGOOD

Quatre. (Four.)

From left to right, James Frawley as CHIEF MAGRUDER,
Arnold Soboloff as TREASURER COOLEY, and Gabriel Dell
as CONTROLLER SCHUB inside the miraculous rock.
Jos. Abeles Studio

Lee Remick and Harry Guardino. *Jos. Abeles Studio*

Angela Lansbury as CORA HOOVER HOOPER celebrates
the miracle. *Jos. Abeles Studio*

BABY JOAN (Jeanne
Tanzy) and that miracu-
lous rock. *Jos. Abeles Studio*

FAY

Bonjour. (Hello.)
    (*She returns*)

HAPGOOD

Voulez-vous monter? (Would you like to come up?)

FAY

Comment? (What?)

HAPGOOD

Monter, monter? (Come up, come up?)
    (FAY *frowns, then steps back to look up at the translation*)

FAY

Ah, oui, oui—monter! Oui, oui. (Ah, yes, yes—come up. Yes, yes.)

HAPGOOD

Pardon: parlez-vous français? (Excuse me: do you speak French?)

FAY

Un peu. (A little.)

HAPGOOD

Anglais? (English?)

FAY

Parfaitement. (Perfectly.)

HAPGOOD

Et puis, vous êtes Américaine. (Then you're an American.)

FAY

Qui n'est pas? (Who isn't?)

HAPGOOD

Et vos cheveux, en votre famille qui a des cheveux rouges?
(And your hair, who in your family has red hair?)

FAY

Personne. (Nobody.)

HAPGOOD

Même pas vous? (Not even you?)

FAY

Même pas moi. C'est une—how do you say? Wig? (Not
even me. It's a—)

HAPGOOD

Wig.

FAY

Do you mind?

HAPGOOD

Not a bit.

FAY

I didn't think you would. (*She sings*) *Docteur, docteur, vous êtes charmant.* (Doctor, doctor, you're charming.)

HAPGOOD

(*Sings*)
Mademoiselle, vous, aussi. (Mademoiselle, you too.)

FAY

(*Sings, keeping French accent*)
You like my hair, yes? My lips, yes?
Ze sway of my—how you say?—of my hips, yes?
You wish to play wiz me?
Okay wiz me,
Come out and play wiz me.
    (*She leaves the balcony*)

HAPGOOD

(*Following*)
Mademoiselle, vous êtes jolie. (Mademoiselle, you're pretty.)

FAY

Docteur, docteur, si gentil. (Doctor, doctor, you're too
    kind.)
You like my style, yes? My brand, yes?
Ze lay of my—how say?—of my land, yes?
You wish to pray wiz me?
To stray wiz me?
Come out and play wiz me.

HAPGOOD

Mademoiselle, vous êtes timide. (Mademoiselle, you're shy.)

FAY

Docteur, docteur, you're so right.
I like your—how you say—
Imperturbable perspicacity.
It's never how you say, it's what you see!

We have ze lark, yes? Ze fling, yes?
Ze play is ze—how you say?—is ze thing, yes?
If you will play wiz me,
Mon chéri,
Though we may not agree
Today
In time—
Mais oui!
We may.

Docteur, docteur, ze English it fails me.
Ah, but, *docteur,* you're good for what ails me.

HAPGOOD

I like your hair—

FAY

Yes?

HAPGOOD

Your lips—

FAY

Yes?

HAPGOOD

Ze sway of your—how you say?—of your hips—

FAY

Yes?

HAPGOOD

Come up and play wiz me.

FAY

Come out and play wiz me.

BOTH

Come on and play wiz me.

FAY

(*Not coming up*)
Docteur, docteur, let's play *docteur* . . .

HAPGOOD

Mademoiselle, you're not well!
But I like your style—

FAY

Yes?

HAPGOOD

Your brand—

FAY

Yes?

HAPGOOD

Ze lay of your—*qu'est-ce que c'est*—of your land—

FAY

Yes?

HAPGOOD

Come up and play wiz me.

FAY

Come out and play wiz me.

BOTH

Come on and play wiz me!

HAPGOOD

(*Gesturing her up*)
Mademoiselle, doctor's orders . . .

FAY

(*Climbing up*)
You're ze *docteur,* I'm impatient . . .

HAPGOOD

You have such—how you say?—unmistakable authen-
ticity!
It isn't how you say, it's what I see!

We have ze lark—yes? Ze fling—yes?
Ze play is ze—how you say?—is ze thing—yes?
  (*During this, she strips off her gloves and her red coat
  so that she is down to a very skimpy, alluring dress.
  Now, she leans back against the proscenium, the
  music becomes satirically seductive, and four gloved
  hands steal out and begin to caress her body.* HAPGOOD
  *gapes and makes a dive for her; she eludes him and
  the owners of the hands appear:* CORA's *four* BOYS.
  During the dance that follows, they keep preventing
  HAPGOOD *from getting to* FAY *who keeps luring him
  on. At last, he does get rid of them and he and* FAY
  end together, singing)

FAY *and* HAPGOOD

Come on and play wiz me,
Mon ami,
Come have your way wiz me
Today!
You play
Wiz me—

HAPGOOD

My way—

FAY

Maybe—

HAPGOOD

Bé-bé—

FAY

Mais oui!

BOTH

We play!

(*After the song, the music resumes softly as* HAPGOOD *leads* FAY *up onto the balcony and through a door, presumably leading to the room inside. The balcony revolves as they come out. He reaches up to the flowered wall panel revealed—and pulls down a short, thin, impractical Murphy bed.* FAY *tries to sit on it seductively but it is hard wood.* HAPGOOD *is trying to get on the bed with her when the telephone rings*)

HAPGOOD

Hello? . . . That is none of your business . . . Well, send up another. (*He hangs up*) It was the management. They wanted to know if you were staying in my room, so I told them to send up—ah! Here it comes now!

(*And another room is riding on; an enormous bed, with glass flowers on the headboard which can light up like a pinball machine when the activity warrants*)

FAY

(*French accent*)
What splendor! A living room—and a loving room!

HAPGOOD

How come you still have the accent?

FAY

It came wiz ze wig.
(*He lies on the big bed, which is very luxurious*)

HAPGOOD

Ah! You know where *you* are? In the living room.

FAY

Bon. Zat is good for discussing ze first reason I am 'ere. Doctor, I 'ave need of your 'elp.

HAPGOOD

(*Cooing*)
It's here: in the loving room.

FAY

Ze loving room . . .

HAPGOOD

Cozy . . .

FAY

Comfortable . . .

HAPGOOD

Come on.

FAY

Chase me.

HAPGOOD

Uh-uh.

FAY

You can catch me.

HAPGOOD

I chased four women in my life—and every one of 'em caught me (*He gets up*) and tried to change me.

FAY

(*Going to him*)

I would not.

HAPGOOD

You're a woman—I adore women.
(*Suddenly, he throws her on the bed in a wild embrace and the flowers light up*)

FAY

And I adore *docteurs*.

HAPGOOD

Médecins. You adore *médecins*.

FAY

Oui. J'adore des médecins parce que je suis une—How do you say "nurse"?

HAPGOOD

You're no nurse—

FAY

I am. (*He laughs. She jumps up*) *Mais oui!* And you are ze *un* doctor who can help me!

HAPGOOD

Come back to the operating table.

FAY

I am *sérieuse!*

HAPGOOD

I'll take you seriously!

FAY

But I am a monster as a nurse! Now—Point—*Une!* (*Music as earlier. She parodies herself*) My name is Apple A-double P-L-E, Fay Apple, qualified head nurse in charge of forty-nine patients in Dr. Detmold's Asylum for the Socially Pressured!
        (*Music holds for*)

HAPGOOD

Oh no, not you!

FAY

Now—Point—*Deux!* (*Music up as before*) Zere is an urgent matter of duty and responsibility and I can never shirk either as I am a dedicated woman of science, control, and—

HAPGOOD

Come here.

FAY

—and order—and—

HAPGOOD

Here.
(*Music becomes a* beguine)

FAY

In order not to identify my beloved Cookies, I am done up
in zis outlandish dress and zis ridiculous wig—

HAPGOOD

Lovely dress, lovely wig—

FAY

And zis lovely wig.
(*She returns to the bed. He begins making love to
her as*)

HAPGOOD

Why the Lady from Lourdes?

FAY

I 'ave come from someplace French.

HAPGOOD

Oui.

FAY

Eh bien! I sink if Madame 'oover 'ooper et Monsieur
Schub, if zey sink I am from Lourdes, per'aps I can frighten

zem into letting my forty-nine Cookies take ze miracle waters.
(*A long kiss; it satisfies both of them; they start to un-
dress*)

HAPGOOD

Why?

FAY

To expose zat miracle as ze fake.

HAPGOOD

What happens if zey find your Cookies first?

FAY

Zey won't. I 'ave stolen ze records which are in my 'andbag.
Which is in ze living room—which is where we better go zis
minute or I will never get you to help me.

HAPGOOD

'Elp.

FAY

'Elp.

HAPGOOD

'Elp you do what?
(*He kisses her*)

FAY

I forgot.

HAPGOOD

I'll do it. Do you believe in miracles?

FAY

No.

HAPGOOD

I do. *One* miracle, anyway.

FAY

Me.

HAPGOOD

(Starting to unzip her dress)

Uh-uh.

FAY

Us.

HAPGOOD

Uh-uh.

FAY

Ow!

(His hand which has been going up her back, pulls at her hair. She shrieks and rolls off the bed)

HAPGOOD

I'm just helping you take your things off.

FAY

(*No accent*)

Not my *hair!*

HAPGOOD

It's not your hair, it's a wig.

FAY

How do you know?

HAPGOOD

You told me!

FAY

I was lying!

HAPGOOD

You're mad!

FAY

It's staying on!

HAPGOOD

I *couldn't* with that thing on!

FAY

(*Scrambling to her feet*)

I couldn't with it off!

HAPGOOD

You probably want the lights off!

FAY

Lights on, wig on!

HAPGOOD

You think if I see you without that damn-fool wig, I won't
want to—

FAY

NO! I won't!!!

HAPGOOD

(After a moment)
You won't?? . . . Oh, nonsense.
(He moves to her)

FAY

(Backing away)
I'm warning you—

HAPGOOD

Nonsense.
(He grabs her, snatches the wig off and kisses her vio-
lently. But she is like a rag doll in his arms. He lets go;
then tests one of her arms; it is rigid. A pause)

FAY

Are you angry?

HAPGOOD

Baffled. Absolutely baffled. Damnedest thing.

FAY

(*Goes to the other room for her red handbag, comb and mirror*)

Eight years ago, at the hospital where I was training, we put on a graduation play. I was what I still am—control and order—so everyone thought it would be funny to make me be a French *soubrette*. This was the dress; zis was ze accent; and (*She holds up the wig*) I put it on; I wore it to the party afterwards. A week later I woke up in a hotel room in Cleveland with an interne.

HAPGOOD

(*Has been dressing*)

A week in a wig—and woe.

FAY

Yes. The wig was off. I was me again and I was shocked.

HAPGOOD

At what?

FAY

Me! Control and order; out the window of that hotel room! Well, I packed that dress *and* that wig *and* that accent; and ever since, wherever I've gone, they've been in a box under my bed. You know how people in AA keep a bottle of whiskey around as a reminder?

HAPGOOD

Think less, enjoy more

FAY

I try. But I just can't let go. Even with that damn wig, it's a struggle. And you can't leave it on. You've got to wash your hair *some*time. And *its* hair.

HAPGOOD

I didn't know you wash a wig.

FAY

Oh sure. I do try! I even had myself psychoanalyzed. By Dr. Detmold.

HAPGOOD

What did you expect?

FAY

A miracle.
        (*A moment. She forces a giggle*)

HAPGOOD

Woman of science?

FAY

I didn't say—

HAPGOOD

        (*Laughs*)
YOU'RE A FAKE! You really *want* your Cookies to take those waters! You hope it really is a miracle!

FAY

Merely because I try to keep an open mind—

HAPGOOD

Merde, mademoiselle! I'll bet you'd like to bathe in those waters yourself!

FAY

All right: yes; I would! For God's sake, I *need* a miracle!

HAPGOOD

Well, there aren't any.

FAY

You said there was one.

HAPGOOD

One you're too complicated to enjoy.

FAY

Oh, am I? What is it?

HAPGOOD

Being alive.

FAY

Oh that.

HAPGOOD

"Oh that." You don't think "that's" a miracle because you don't understand human nature. We are all out to do each other in, and if we're not celebrating victory tomorrow, it'll be Miracle Number Two. "Oh that." We're never present at the end of "oh that" so we never know what it means—if anything. All we *do* know about "oh that," Nurse A-double P-L-E, is we have it; and the only thing we can do is enjoy it—*now!*

FAY

Wait; I'll put on the wig!

HAPGOOD

That'd be like taking advantage of a drunk.

FAY

Take advantage!

HAPGOOD

Go home to your asylum.

FAY

No!—Listen, I'll get drunk!

HAPGOOD

I'll bet you can't.

FAY

I can't . . . I can't be hypnotized. I can't laugh—not really. I can't whistle—

HAPGOOD

Nonsense.

FAY

No, true. I can't sing at parties. I can't play the piano by
ear. When I was little, my, how I wanted to! My girl friend
could. Once I walked into a music store, sat down at a big,
shiny grand piano—and I played. (*Terrible sounds from pit
piano*) Well, you can take piano lessons. Use a metronome;
learn control and order. (*Scales on pit piano, turning into
lead-in for the song*) But . . . you can't take lessons in whis-
tling. So—your woman of science; every walk I take, every
street, every year, I wait. My mouth waits. But—(*Her mouth
puckers*) I can't.

 (*She sings*)
Anyone can whistle,
That's what they say—
 Easy.
Anyone can whistle
Any old day—
 Easy.
It's all so simple:
Relax, let go, let fly.
So someone tell me why
 Can't I?
I can dance a tango,
I can read Greek—
 Easy.
I can slay a dragon
Any old week—
 Easy.
What's hard is simple,
What's natural comes hard.
Maybe you could show me
 How to let go,
 Lower my guard,
 Learn to be free.

Maybe if you whistle,
    Whistle for me.
    (*The music continues softly as* HAPGOOD *goes to her
    and kisses her gently. Even though she tries to re-
    spond, she goes rigid again, and he moves away*)

HAPGOOD

I thought perhaps that week in Cleveland—

FAY

(*Sadly*)
It was a helluva week in Cleveland . . . But I was wearing
that wig and—

HAPGOOD

I know.
    (*He smiles nicely at her, turns away and goes back to
    the bed as she reprises the last half of the song. At the
    end, they are apart from each other. The lights dim
    out and both beds slide off into the darkness. A mo-
    ment, then the march from the opening of the act
    strikes up and the lights come up on the town square.
    The two Groups are parading, carrying their placards
    and singing lustily. During their marching, the re-
    verse side of their signs is shown and all are exactly
    the same: all bear the one word YES on the same
    colored background*)

GROUP A

Hooray for Hapgood,
Hapgood can be trusted,
Friend of the well-adjusted in Group A!

GROUP ONE

Hooray for Hapgood,
Play a part with Hapgood,
Miracles start with Hapgood,
Gladden your heart with Hapgood!

BOTH

Join the parade with Hapgood!
No one's afraid with Hapgood!

Follow your star with Hapgood!
Know who you are with Hapgood!

Throw in your lot for Hapgood!
Everyone's hot for Hapgood!
> (CORA *emerges through the singing marchers waving a chiffon handkerchief. She gets shoved around a bit and sings out to them, as they march by, ignoring her*)

CORA

Hi! . . . Hey! . . . Wait! . . . Voters . . .
> (*They are gone; she is alone, and she sings quietly*)

I see flags, I hear bells,
There's a parade in town.
I see crowds, I hear yells,
There's a parade in town!

I hear drums in the air,
I see clowns in the square,
I see marchers marching,
Tossing hats at the sky.

Did you hear? Did you see?
Is a parade in town?
Are there drums without me?
Is a parade in town?
Well, they're out of step, the flutes are squeaky, the
    banners are frayed.
Any parade in town without me
Must be a second class parade!

So! . . . Ha! . . .
> (*But the marchers storm on again, singing loudly and
> paying no attention to her*)

BOTH GROUPS

Hapgood has no answers or suggestions,
Only a lot of questions.
We like questions!
What's the use of answers or suggestions?
As long as we're told where to go,
There isn't a thing we need to know.
> (*They start to repeat their original refrains, but* CORA
> *claps her hands over her ears, shutting them out as
> she sings until they have marched off and she is
> alone*)

CORA

Did you hear? Did you see?
Was a parade in town?
Were there drums without me?
Was a parade in town?
Cause I'm dressed at last, at my best, and my banners are
    high
Tell me, while I was getting ready
Did a parade go by?
> (*She stands bewildered, forlorn:* SCHUB *enters*)

SCHUB

I know: they hate you.

CORA

And they love him!

SCHUB

Oh, everybody loves a pretty face. And the rabble worships anyone who tells 'em they belong to anything.

CORA

(*Pacing*)
They belong to *me*—and they were carrying him on *my* litter.

SCHUB

(*He too paces furiously*)
If he weren't a psychiatrist, I'd swear he knew what he was doing.

CORA

I should be on their backs!

SCHUB

He's turned the whole town into a madhouse! We're on the brink of a disaster!

CORA

It's *my* disaster!

SCHUB

Madam, will you forget yourself for the moment?

CORA

I only live for the moment.

SCHUB

Well, at this moment we must stop every single person from taking those waters until those damn Cookies are locked up.

CORA

Why?

SCHUB

Otherwise Hapgood or some other anarchist will say an epidemic of lunacy was caused by our miracle.

CORA

Oh my God! We'll be ruined by our saviour! Quick!

SCHUB

What?

CORA

Here!

SCHUB

Where?

CORA

Somewhere, something, somebody! *SCHUB! COMP-TROL—*

SCHUB

I'm here.

CORA

Don't panic.

SCHUB

Don't you panic.

CORA

But we must do something!

SCHUB

Of course, we must do something!

CORA

I am doing something.

SCHUB

What?

CORA

I'm panicking.

SCHUB

So am I.

BOTH

(*A shriek*)

POLICE!

CORA

Ah, There's nothing like a good scream.

SCHUB

Yes, I feel much better. Now: a quick way to destroy that damn doctor's popularity.

CORA

Is that absolutely necessary?

SCHUB

My dear girl—

CORA

(*A deep breath*)

All right, Schub.

SCHUB

All right what?

CORA

I'll marry him. (*He looks at her. Weakly*) Just a—tiny bit of humor.

SCHUB

(*Wistfully*)

Not everybody loves a pretty face.

CORA

(*Gently*)

You have charm, Schub.

SCHUB
(*Sweetly*)
Your place or mine?

CORA

Mine. I'm getting a massage.

MAGRUDER
(*Runs on with* COOLEY)
Your honor!

SCHUB

I told you to guard the miracle!

MAGRUDER

I got a posse of special deputies around the rock.

COOLEY

Brother, it'll take more than deputies to keep that crowd from taking the waters.

CORA
(*Sings* a capella)
Schub! Comptroller Schub!

SCHUB

No need to panic, dear lady. I'll think of a plan to save us.

CORA
(*Charming steel*)
Of course you will. After all, a man who is capable of inventing a miracle is capable of anything. (*He kisses her*

hand) Seven-thirty. My house. (*She starts off, then turns back)* All of you.

    (*She exits*)

SCHUB

By God, gentlemen, there's a woman who can handle a crowd!

    (*And the crowd of marchers returns, singing away as* SCHUB, COOLEY *and* MAGRUDER *stride off. As the marchers parade around and off, the "living room" and the "loving room" come back on.* HAPGOOD *is lying across the big bed, watching* FAY *put her wig back on. The contents of her red traveling bag are strewn around her—including the stolen records)*

HAPGOOD

It's damn depressing: watching a woman get dressed after you didn't.

FAY

It's time to charge City Hall.

HAPGOOD

Where's the accent?

FAY

No point in wasting it here. Are you coming?

HAPGOOD

You know, with or without that wig, you're almost beautiful.

FAY

I'm not a real beauty and I'm glad.

HAPGOOD

Why?

FAY

Because I never have to worry about becoming an ex-beauty.

HAPGOOD

Bonjour.

FAY

Hello; and come on.

HAPGOOD

I said *Bonjour.*

FAY

And I said Hello. (*She look at him; then*) Oh, Hell!! (*She hurls herself into his arms*) Bon-jour!
          (*A wild kiss*)

HAPGOOD

It's that nurse who gets in the way.

FAY

Oui.

HAPGOOD

What're we going to do about her?

FAY

Kiss her.

HAPGOOD

Are these her records?

FAY

Oui.

HAPGOOD

Tear 'em up.

FAY

What??

HAPGOOD

What's the easiest way to get rid of a nurse? Get rid of her patients. Tear 'em up!

FAY

That's tearing up people.

HAPGOOD

Most people'd like to be torn up and set free. You'd love it!

FAY

I would not!
     (*She starts gathering up records frantically*)

HAPGOOD

And your Cookies would, too! They could stop pretending

to be like everybody else and go back to living the way they want; they could enjoy!

FAY

And end up right back in the asylum again!

HAPGOOD

So what? We're all going to end up dead; why lie down and fold up now?! (*Stopping her*) Fay, the world made those Cookies, you didn't. Fix the world, not them! Come on, lady: tear 'em up! (*He grabs a record*) Let 'em go! Let yourself go!

FAY

I couldn't.

HAPGOOD

It's easy.

FAY

No.

HAPGOOD

I'll show you how.
     (*He holds up record to rip it*)

FAY

Don't!

HAPGOOD

Are you protesting or do you mean it?

I mean it. Don't.

HAPGOOD

(*Contemptuously drops record on bed as music starts. He sings low, with tight anger at first, then with mounting passion*)
Everybody says don't,
Everybody says don't,
Everybody says don't—it isn't right,
Don't—it isn't nice!

Everybody says don't,
Everybody says don't,
Everybody says don't walk on the grass,
Don't disturb the peace,
Don't skate on the ice.

Well, I
Say
Do.
I say
Walk on the grass, it was meant to feel!
I
Say
Sail!
Tilt at the windmill,
And if you fail, you fail.

Everybody says don't,
Everybody says don't,
Everybody says don't get out of line
    When they say that, then,
Lady, that's a sign:

Nine times out of ten,
Lady, you are doing just fine!

Make just a ripple.
Come on, be brave.
This time a ripple,
Next time a wave.
Sometimes you have to start small,
Climbing the tiniest wall,
Maybe you're going to fall—
But it's better than not starting at all!

Everybody says no,
Everybody says stop,
Everybody says mustn't rock the boat!
Mustn't touch a thing!

Everybody says don't,
Everybody says wait,
Everybody says can't fight City Hall,
Can't upset the cart,
Can't laugh at the King!

Well, I
Say
Try!
I
Say
Laugh at the kings, or they'll make you cry.
Lose
Your
Poise!
Fall if you have to,
But, lady, make a noise!

Everybody says don't.
Everybody says can't.
Everybody says wait around for miracles,
That's the way the world is made!
I insist on
Miracles, if *you* do them,
Miracles—nothing to them!
I say don't:
Don't be afraid!
> (*He holds up the record and reads*)

"Engels, David J."
> (*A moment. He starts to rip it; she snatches it from him*)

FAY

I don't know what kind of a doctor you are but I'm a registered nurse and I cannot allow you to tear up my patients.

HAPGOOD

I'm no kind of doctor.

FAY

> (*Putting record away*)

That's right: pout.

HAPGOOD

I'm not pouting, I am merely telling you I am not a doctor.

FAY

What do you mean you're not a doctor?

HAPGOOD

I mean I'm not a doctor.

FAY

You certainly are a doctor. You're Dr. J. Bowden Hapgood.

HAPGOOD

I am J. Bowden Hapgood but I am not now, nor have I ever been a member of the medical profession. I've never even been sick.

FAY

But everybody knows—

HAPGOOD

Everybody knows whatever they're told.

FAY

But you said—

HAPGOOD

(Goes for his coat)

I said? I said "Doctor," that's all. I came here by train, escorted by a very charming if slightly overly-attached gentleman. Before we got to the asylum, we were met by a very amiable if slightly alcoholic nurse. She in turn escorted me to your very gracious if slightly befuddled boss. *She* said "Doctor"—*he* said "Doctor"—(*He extends his hand*) I said "Doctor"—(*He extends his other hand*) And there I was: Dr. J. Bowden Hapgood.

(*He shakes hands with himself*)

FAY

Then you're—

HAPGOOD

Dear Nurse Apple—
(*He reaches into the coat pocket*)

FAY

Oh no.

HAPGOOD

(*Pulls out a record identical to the others and presents it*)
—I am your fiftieth Cookie.

FAY

You're crazy!

HAPGOOD

(*Beams*)
And you have to take care of me. Read it. But don't tear *me*
up because I love being a Cookie and I want to stay in your
lovely Jar.

FAY

(*Reading from the record*)
"Hapgood, J. Bowden. Professor of Statistical Philosophy."
Four, no, five degrees! Adviser to the President"!

HAPGOOD

Until late one recession when it dawned on me you can use
any figures to prove any side of any question.

FAY

What'd you do?

HAPGOOD

Quit.

FAY

And then?

HAPGOOD

Then? . . . I followed the seasons around the world.

FAY

(*Softly*)

Oh my Hapgood!

HAPGOOD

Not quite so fast. (*He points to the record*) I've been arrested.

FAY

(*Admiringly*)

Seventeen times!

HAPGOOD

A hundred and seventeen. Machines are getting to be as bad as people.

FAY

Why were you arrested?

HAPGOOD

For trying to keep the miracle going.

FAY

How?

HAPGOOD

In a hundred and seventeen different ways. Once I held an aquacade off a testing island. That was my hundredth arrest. Then day before yesterday, I went to the UN—and played "Auld Lang Syne" on my horn.

FAY

What horn?

HAPGOOD

My trumpet. (*He produces it from the small oblong case he arrived with*) I thought it was loud enough to waken the dying. Turns out I'm only the Pied Piper for lunatics. So that trumpet goes under *my* bed.

FAY

How can they say you're crazy! You're a musician!

HAPGOOD

I only play by ear.

FAY

Oh, darling!

HAPGOOD

But they're right! Until this morning, I was probably the

craziest man in the world. Because I was not only an idealist, I was a practising idealist! Now *that is mad;* it's thankless; and it's absolutely exhausting! (*He looks at her, smiles*) Smile: it's finished. I'm free now!

FAY

Free? (*Holds up his record*) You lunatic, you've been certified! You've been committed!

HAPGOOD

Yes, isn't it marvelous! I'm not responsible to or for anything or anyone. I'm a retired Don Quixote!

FAY

. . . Then why have you been trying to help me?

HAPGOOD

Oh—for fun . . . (*She keeps staring*) Habit. And a bad one . . . A hangover from yesterday . . . Well, I can't just turn it off in one day!

FAY

I don't think you can turn it off at all!

HAPGOOD

But I'm mad, I'm crazy, I'm insane!
> (*On this, he grabs his coat, jumps over the beds and ends in a madman-like pose with the coat over his head.* FAY *looks at him with loving admiration and says softly*)

FAY

You're marvelous. (*A moment; then he removes the coat,*

straightens up and stares at this girl who believes in him. She goes for her records and holds up the one he started to tear) "Engels, David J."
    (Holds it out to him)

HAPGOOD

It's on your head.

FAY

It's your miracle.

HAPGOOD

It's anybody's.

FAY

. . . Even—mine?

HAPGOOD

Could be.

FAY

"Engels, David J."
    (Music, and a spotlight picks out Engels who stands quite still with the "Cookie" grin on his face, waiting to be freed. The two rooms begin to disappear, HAPGOOD riding off with them as he urges:)

HAPGOOD

Well, come on! Do it!
    (FAY hesitates and then with a surge of music, rips the record, setting Engels free. He stops his grin and begins to dance. This is the beginning of a ballet in

which FAY *rips up the records of the* COOKIES, *setting them free, in dance, to be what they want. As each gets free, he infects other people who pick up what he is doing. Until, at last,* FAY *herself is infected and begins to dance freely and happily. At the climax,* HAPGOOD *appears on the balcony of the hotel. Everyone clears but* FAY *who is across the stage from him. A brief moment, then she slowly begins to walk across the stage to him, with her hands outstretched to him as*

The Curtain Falls

ACT THREE

(CORA *is stretched out on a massage table in her solarium getting a massage from one of the four* BOYS. *She sings out, a capella, as usual*)
  Schub! Comptroller Schub!
    (COOLEY *enters: his eyebrows and hands go up at the spectacle of her body on the table*)

COOLEY

He isn't here yet.

CORA

I know he isn't here yet. It comforts me to call him.

COOLEY

Good for you, Sister!
    (*He starts to massage her. The masseur gets resentful and works harder;* CORA *remains oblivious*)

CORA

But where is he? Where is his plan to save me? Oh, I'm depressed! NO! (COOLEY *removes his hands*) Cora Hoover Hooper will not be depressed!

COOLEY

Right you are, Sister!
    (*Back go his hands*)

CORA

It's out of character. My newspaper always comments on my joy, my gaiety, my God! To think of Hapgood and that Lady from Lourdes joining forces in adjoining rooms! Oh, Cooley, pray she's too religious!

COOLEY

What's the good of praying? She's French.

MAGRUDER

(*Hurrying in*)
Reporting in, Your Honor.
(*His mouth drops open at the sight of the double massage*)

CORA

(*Salutes him, then*)
Where's Schub? Where's his plan? Magruder, will you shut your mouth and answer me?

MAGRUDER

The comptroller's on his way over.
(*Now he begins to massage Cora: all three masseurs are working in the same rhythm. She appears not to notice*)

CORA

Heaven! Schub will save me; he's brilliant. I'm attracted to brilliant men. The late Harvey Hoover Hooper was brilliant —in a rather stupid way, of course.

SCHUB

(*He enters*)

Dear Mayor-ess—

CORA

Dear Comptroller—(*She holds out her free hand for him to kiss. He does and begins to massage her arm. Now all four men are massaging her in rhythm*) You're here!

SCHUB

I am!

CORA

And the plan?

SCHUB

I have it.

CORA

What is it?

SCHUB

You resign.

CORA

I resign. (*Now realizing what it means*) I resign?! EVERY-BODY—OFF! (*On this, she pushes out with hands and feet, shoving the four masseurs away from her. Another of the four* BOYS *enters with negligee and shoes which she puts on while she screams at* SCHUB *and the others*) I resign? I resign?

SCHUB

Well, it *is* your administration that's in trouble—

CORA

My administration—you're putting the shoe on the wrong foot, you poop! I don't resign for one minute, Comptroller Schub! But you're fired. You're all fired. No, no, you're demoted. To Dog Catcher. Dog Catcher Schub, that's the job for a man like you. Man? (*She is dressed and raging about like a tigress now. The massage table and the two* BOYS *have gone*) Harvey Hoover Hooper was a man but his breed died with him! No wonder you have a lady mayor, you male impersonators! Well, guard the governor's mansion! Guard the White House! You're finished and I'm taking over! STOP THE MIRACLE!

COOLEY

Now, Sister—

CORA

Don't "sister" me, Sister! I said Stop the Miracle!

MAGRUDER

How?

CORA

By turning off the water, you nymphomaniac! The three of you have got exactly fifteen minutes in which to do it and to get that machinery out of the pumphouse or you go to jail. I am not going to have a scandal in my administration because when I run for Governor—

COOLEY

But Sister, Your Honor—

CORA

And President—

COOLEY

But you have just saved us!

CORA

. . . What?

COOLEY

If there is no water, there's no miracle. And if there's no miracle, there's nothing for that Lady from Lourdes to investigate!

MAGRUDER

She'll go home!

COOLEY

Right!

CORA

—*I'm brilliant!* But that still leaves Dr. Hapgood—

MAGRUDER

And the town.

COOLEY

Oh Sistren and Brethren, if we can just show the people

the evil of Dr. Hapgood's ways, they'll be normal and frightened—like they used to be—

CORA

And they'll do as I say. Cooley, *you're* brilliant. Now: how
do we get them to turn against Hapgood? (COOLEY's *happy
face falls; she pushes him away*) Washout. (*She turns and
sees* SCHUB. *A little girl smile comes over her face and very
sweetly, she croons*) Schub? *Comptroller* Schub?
> (*He turns and looks at her. She lowers herself into a
> deep curtsey. Gallantly, he takes her hand, raises her
> and holds her in an embrace*)

SCHUB

All right: now.

CORA

Now?

COOLEY

(*Firmly*)

Now.
> (*They all begin to pace, music enters and continues
> throughout the scene which is part rhythmic dia-
> logue, part song*)

MAGRUDER

Now what?

SCHUB

(*Sings*)
Now why did the miracle go dry?

MAGRUDER

(*Sings*)

'Cause we turned the water off, is why.

CORA

Idiot!

SCHUB

Fool!

COOLEY

Oaf!

SCHUB

Moron!

CORA

Idiot!

SCHUB

Dolt!

CORA

IDIOT!

SCHUB

(*Sings*)

We didn't turn it off, you see,
'Cause we didn't turn it on, not *we* . . .

MAGRUDER

Who did?

SCHUB

(After a moment, beaming)

He did.

CORA

Who did?

COOLEY

He did?

MAGRUDER

You did?

SCHUB

(Points upward)

He did.

OTHERS

(The light dawns; singing)

He did!
Just what we just what we just what we needed!

SCHUB

(Sings)

Now why did He turn it off so quick?
A sign that our little town is sick.

CORA

Brilliant!

MAGRUDER

Good.

COOLEY

Clever.

CORA
(Shoots him a look)
Brilliant.

COOLEY

Brilliant.

SCHUB
(Sings)
Sick people running wild, no less.
And who is responsible?
    (Smiling slowly)
One guess.

MAGRUDER

Who is?

CORA
(Catching on, slowly)
Doctor Hapgood.

COOLEY

(*Faster*)

Doctor Hapgood.

MAGRUDER

(*Faster*)

Doctor Hapgood!

ALL

(*Singing joyfully*)

Doctor Hapgood! Doctor Hapgood! Doctor Hapgood!
Hallelujah, Brother, cheers and acclaim!
Hallelujah, we've got someone to blame!
Hallelujah, Praise the Lord and Amen!

CORA

Schub, you've done it again.
    (*The clinging vine*)
Whenever my world falls apart,
I never lose hope or lose heart.
Whatever the form
    Of the storm
    That may brew,
I've got you to lean on.
When everything's hopelessly gray,
You'll notice I'm youthfully gay!
There isn't a sing-
    Le great thing
    I can't do,
Not with you to lean on,
Darling you!

With you to depend on, I'll never quit.

There isn't a murder I couldn't commit.
I look like a love-
> Ly girl of
> Twenty-two!

I've got you to lean on!

SCHUB

> (*Leaning on* COOLEY)

I've got you to lean on!

COOLEY

> (*Leaning on* MAGRUDER)

I've got you to lean on!
> (MAGRUDER *looks around in vain, starts to open his mouth, but* SCHUB *resumes pacing*)

SCHUB

> (*Sings*)

Now how do we educate the mass?

MAGRUDER

> (*Sings*)

With hoses and tommy-guns and gas.

CORA

Idiot!

SCHUB

Fool!

COOLEY

Oaf!

SCHUB

Moron!

CORA

Idiot!

SCHUB

Dolt!

CORA

IDIOT!

SCHUB
(Sings)
Can't tear a hero down by force.
So how do we educate—
    (Beaming, slowly)
Of course—

MAGRUDER

How?

SCHUB

Smear him.

CORA

Smear him?

COOLEY

Smear him . . .

MAGRUDER

Spear him?

SCHUB

Smear him.

OTHERS

(*Singing*)

Smear him!
No one'll no one'll no one'll hear him!

SCHUB

(*Sings*)

Now what can we label him, my friends?
A phrase that the rabble comprehends . . .

COOLEY

"Religious pervert."

MAGRUDER

Brilliant!

CORA

Terrible!

MAGRUDER

(*Hastily*)

Terrible!

CORA

Idiot.

SCHUB

(*Sings*)
A phrase with a little more finesse . . .
Obscene but inspiring—
     (*Smiling, slowly*)
Ah, yes—

MAGRUDER

Yes?

SCHUB

"Enemy of Heaven."

CORA

"—Heaven . . ."

COOLEY

"—Heaven . . ."

MAGRUDER

"—Heaven . . ."

CORA

Heaven!

MEN

(*Sing*)

Enemy of God,
Enemy of the Church,
Enemy of Heaven!

CORA

(*Sings*)

I didn't hear it,
But spread it.
I never said it,
But spread it!

ALL

(*Sing*)

Hallelujah, all our problems are through!
Hallelujah, that's what teamwork can do!
Hallelujah, Brothers, pull on the oars!

CORA

Schub, my kingdom is yours.
    (*Clinging, as before*)
Whenever my world turns to dust,
I've always got someone to trust.
Whatever the sort
    Of support
    That I need,
I've got you to lean on.

MEN

When everything's hollow and black,
You'll always have us at your back.
    (CORA *does a take*)
No matter how hollow,
    We'll follow
    Your lead—
And with us to lean on,
You'll succeed!

CORA

What comfort it is to have always known
That if they should catch me, I won't go alone.
   I'll always give credit
      Where credit
      Is due—
I've got you to lean on!

MEN

We've got you to lean on!

CORA

      (*Shakes her head, lovingly*)
I've got *you* to lean on—
      (*They all start a vaudeville exit, music continuing
      under*)

SCHUB

Once *he's* out of the way . . .

CORA

And *she's* out of the way . . .

SCHUB

Our miracle is working again . . .
      (*He exits*)

COOLEY

We're back in business . . .
      (*He exits*)

MAGRUDER

(*Pointing up*)

And *he* turns off the water.

(*He exits*)

CORA

Idiot.

(CORA *doublecrosses the men by not exiting with
them. Instead, joined by the four* BOYS *who come
sneaking on from the opposite side, she goes into a
joyful tap dance with them which ends with them
throwing her on the massage table and wheeling her
off madly but triumphantly. Blackout.*

*When the lights come up, they are rather dim. We
are in the town square and the rock is slowly sliding
on.* SCHUB, COOLEY *and* MAGRUDER *enter quietly.*
SCHUB *looks up at the water, gives* MAGRUDER *a pat
on the back and* MAGRUDER *disappears behind the
rock. Music has begun a slow beat under this and
continues as a* TOWNSMAN *enters.* SCHUB *begins to
whisper to him and then points to the water—which
suddenly has stopped.* SCHUB *wanders off as the*
TOWNSMAN *stares and runs off.* COOLEY *has begun to
impart the same news to a woman. Other people come
on; the news is passed along; the first* TOWNSMAN *returns with some others. More and more people run
on, look at the place where the water used to be; whisper to each other. Then, against the steadily building
music, they begin to chant*)

CROWD

Hapgood. Hapgood! HAPGOOD! HAPGOOD! *HAP-
GOOD!!*

(*At the peak of the chant, the music cuts off and there is dead silence as* HAPGOOD *and* FAY *come out of the hotel. The smile leaves* HAPGOOD's *face as he realizes this is not the admiring crowd who cheered him before.* MRS. SCHROEDER *makes her way forward to him*)

MRS. SCHROEDER

All right, Doctor . . . who's loony?

HAPGOOD

(*Charm*)

All of us.

MRS. SCHROEDER

(*Patient but hard*)

Doctor—*which* are the loonies?

FAY

Now—hear—this!

HAPGOOD

(*Stopping her*)

Mademoiselle feels that inasmuch as we are all children of heaven—

MAN

Shut up. We know about you.

HAPGOOD

You know what about—

MRS. SCHROEDER

Blasphemer! Which are your loony patients?

HAPGOOD

They're all gone.

MRS. SCHROEDER

Then where's our miracle? (*Percussion starts*) Name your patients, Doctor.

HAPGOOD

(*Charm*)
I never had any. I'm not even a doctor.

MAN

Come on! We want those loonies back in the bin.

MRS. SCHROEDER

We want our miracle!

HAPGOOD

Look—

MRS. SCHROEDER

Are you going to tell us?

MAN

We'll make him tell!
        (*Interrogation music starts, darkly*)

HAPGOOD

(*To* SCHROEDER)

Watchcry!

MRS. SCHROEDER

(*Pointing at him*)

Enemy of the church!

HAPGOOD

(*Wheeling*)

Watchcry!

MAN

(*Pointing*)

Enemy of Heaven!

HAPGOOD

Watchcry!

SECOND MAN

(*Pointing*)

Enemy of God! *Get him!*

(*The crowd has slowly been edging closer. Now, as the music breaks out, they break out and go for* HAPGOOD *and* FAY. *The only escape is over the rock and* HAPGOOD *takes* FAY's *hand and drags her up onto the rock which begins to revolve as the lights go down and the music gets louder. When the lights come up full, the rock has revolved and* FAY *and* HAPGOOD *are running into the cave. The pump and the hoseline for the water have been covered with old burlap.* HAPGOOD *starts to peer around as* FAY *rages*)

FAY

Ingrates. Traitors. Turncoats. Turntails. Rats. Finks!

HAPGOOD

(*Grins*)

Apostates

FAY

And after the way they worshipped you!

HAPGOOD

That's par for people. What is this place?

FAY

A cave left over from the Peer Gynt Festival. I don't understand you. You expect the worst and you hope for the best.

HAPGOOD

It's protection. And sometimes (*He takes her in his arms*) I get the best.

FAY

Blushing doesn't suit this wig.

HAPGOOD

Well, you'd better leave it on or you'll be recognized and arrested—and you'll have to identify your Cookies.

FAY

Never!

HAPGOOD

Never say that until you've—
(*He has been following the trail of a wire which has led him to the pump switch. He flicks it and now the burlap covering the pump begins to jiggle crazily. Bells peal out. As* HAPGOOD *yanks down the burlap and he and* FAY *see what the cave has been used for, there are cries and joyful yells from offstage. The door to the cave opens and* CORA *enters. She turns and calls out*)

CORA

Hold that mob at bay! (*Then, seeing* HAPGOOD *with* FAY *in his arms*) Doctor! What's been going on in here?

SCHUB

(*Enters*)
What's been going on in here?

CORA

Oh, stop asking damn fool questions. (SCHUB *shuts the cave door*) It's perfectly obvious what's been going on in here.

HAPGOOD

It certainly is.

SCHUB

Our miracles, my dear *mademoiselle*—(*He rips wires out: pump stops; noise outside stops*)—are a bit different from yours.

CORA

Oh, Schub!

SCHUB

This one is not going to work again until our dear doctor is run out of town.

FAY

(*To* CORA *and* SCHUB, *with the accent*)
You miserable, low, dirty—

MAGRUDER

(*Runs in*)
Your Honor, they're getting restless! Should we open fire?

CORA

Yes—on France!

MAGRUDER

Right!
    (*He turns and crashes into a* TELEGRAPH BOY *with a long white beard who runs in*)

TELEGRAPH BOY

Telegram for Her Honor, the Mayor-ess!

CORA

(*To* MAGRUDER)
Clumsy! Have you no respect for the aged?
    (MAGRUDER *goes as* CORA *passes the telegram to* SCHUB *who reads it*)

TELEGRAPH BOY

(*Nudging* CORA)
It's from the Governor.

CORA

(*Proudly*)

Ah!

SCHUB

Not exactly. (*Reading*) "Mayor-ess Cora Hoover Hooper: unless your quota of forty-nine patients is behind bars by sundown, you will be impeached."

CORA

(A capella)

Schub!

SCHUB

I'm here.

CORA

I'm finished.

SCHUB

Never say die.

CORA

I'd rather die than be dumped!

SCHUB

Dear lady, use my head. Forty-nine patients are as good as behind bars right this minute.

CORA

They are?! Where are they?

SCHUB

We can pick and choose from anybody in town—thanks to you, dear Doctor.

HAPGOOD

At your service, dear Comptroller. What have I done?

SCHUB

Group A? Group One? No difference between them; all mad as hatters? You've already certified them. All we need do is commit them.

CORA

Brilliant!

HAPGOOD

Touché!

FAY

No!

CORA

No?????

FAY

You cannot just pick people up off ze streets and lock zem up!

CORA

I can do anything I want! (*To* SCHUB) What do we need? A mere forty-nine patients! That's twenty head of males—no, *ten* head of males and thirty-nine head of females!

SCHUB

We'll just round them up and lock them up.

CORA

What a sweet ring that has to it! Schub-chen, you're a genius!

HAPGOOD

I salute you! Both of you! King and Queen of Madmen!

CORA

No: President and First Gentleman. *En garde, mademoiselle.* You have seventeen minutes to leave town—or I'll lock *you* up as an unregistered foreign agent. Schub!

SCHUB

Your Honor—

CORA

Allez-y!
(*And they exit grandly as* HAPGOOD *bows like a courtier*)

FAY

You salute them?

HAPGOOD

Sure

FAY

They're mad.

HAPGOOD

Very. But they were driven into a corner.

FAY

Who hasn't been?

HAPGOOD

And look at you, with that wig. Look at me! How else do you get out of corners? Either you die slowly or you have the strength to go crazy.

FAY

But what that pair of madmen is going to do is frightening! And we can stop them so easily by telling the town about that pump.

HAPGOOD

You might as well tell them there is no God.

FAY

But we *know* that miracle is a fake.

HAPGOOD

But it *works*, Fay. It works like any miracle!

FAY

For the moment!

HAPGOOD

That's all they want it for! They need it! You can lead

them by the hand into this cave, show them that electric pump, and they will still say: it's a miracle!

FAY

SO SALUTE! So do nothing!

HAPGOOD

Why not?

FAY

You can't die slowly!

HAPGOOD

Maybe not, but I can vegetate! Look, I was granted your asylum and I intend to enjoy it. Until the staff returns, I am going back to my hotel, sit on my balcony and watch life in the square.

FAY

You can't. I won't let you!

HAPGOOD

Fay, I AM NO DOCTOR FOR THIS COCKEYED WORLD!

FAY

But you're *my* doctor!

HAPGOOD

Then, I'm a bad doctor for you—because you've become as crazy as I *was*.

FAY

So to hell with me!
> (*She slaps him across the face and rushes away from
> him furiously. All the lights go out except a spot on
> her as she sings angrily*)

Take one step
And see what it gets you,
See what it gets you,
See what it gets you!
One step up
And see how it gets you
Down.
Give yourself,
If somebody lets you—
See what it gets you,
See what it gets you!
Give yourself
And somebody lets you
Down.

Here's how to crawl
Now run, lady!
Here's how to walk
Now fly!
Here's how to feel—have fun, lady,
And a fond goodbye!

Reach out your hand
And see what it gets you,
See what it gets you,
See what it gets you!
Trouble is, whatever it gets,
You find
That once you see, you can't stay blind.

What do I do now,
Now that my eyes are wide?
Well, when the world goes mad, then they've got to be
    shown,
And when the hero quits then you're left on your own,
And when you want things done, you have to do them
    yourself alone!
And if I'm not ready
And light-headed,
I can't stand here dumb.
So, ready or not, here—I hope—I come!

Anyone can whistle, that's what they say—easy.
Anyone can whistle any old day—easy.
It's all so simple: relax, let go, let fly.
And someone tell me why can't I?
Whistle at a dragon: down it'll fall—easy.
Whistle at a hero, trumpets and all—easy.
Just once I'll do it,
Just once before I die.
Lead me to the battle,
What does it take?
Over the top!
Joan at the stake!
Anyone can whistle—
        (*She tries, unsuccessfully*)
Well, no one can say
I didn't try!
        (*There is a blackout. In the darkness, the sound of a
        police whistle and the lights come up on the town
        square where police* DEPUTIES *are rushing back and
        forth with small machine guns, getting in each other's
        way and upsetting* MAGRUDER *who is directing
        others as they wheel on a large animal cage. Over all
        this, we hear* CORA's *voice enormously amplified:*)

CORA (Off)

PLACES, EVERYONE! IT'S LOCK UP TIME! SYN-
CHRONIZE YOUR WATCHES! SURROUND THE
SQUARE!

> (DR. DETMOLD *has come on and stands by the door
> to the cage with a hospital clipboard in his hand. An-
> other "civilian" has wandered on: an* OLD LADY *with a
> shopping bag full of vegetables. She is watching the
> activities with a touch of interest and pleasure when:*)

CORA (Off)

ARREST THAT CRAZY LADY! (MRS. SCHROEDER
wanders on; the DEPUTIES *make a dive for her*) NO, NOT
MRS. SCHROEDER! THE OTHER CRAZY LADY!
SHE'S A FUGITIVE FROM THE COOKIE JAR!

> (*The* OLD LADY *has been looking around for the
> "other crazy lady" when the* DEPUTIES *descend on
> her, surround her and shove her into a pastel-colored
> straitjacket. There is dead silence, and then* CORA
> *sweeps on in a chic but bizarre version of a deputy's
> uniform*)

CORA

Well done, gentlemen! From now, I expect every man
among you to be—*on—your—toes!*

> (*And as the lights brighten and the music starts, that
> is precisely where the* DEPUTIES *get: every one of
> them stands on point! Even the* OLD LADY *is up on
> point, for this is the beginning of the Cookie Chase,
> a sequence wherein* CORA, *her cohorts and the
> DEPUTIES lock up anybody in town they can get
> their hands on. It is all done to waltz music in the
> style of classical ballet short variations, punctuated by
> someone being thrown into or released from the cage*)

CORA

(*Sings, as* DEPUTIES *promenade with the* OLD LADY)
Lock 'em up! Put 'em away
In The Jar!
Time to start getting the nets out!
Lock 'em up
Into the cage!
Quietly: no one must know.
Cart 'em off into the bin;
Turn the key
Quick before anyone gets out!
Turn the key, throw it away,
There we are: forty-eight to go!
> (*On this last, she points to the* OLD LADY *who has
> been captured in an arabesque by two* DEPUTIES.
> *The music continues as*)

CORA

Detmold.

DETMOLD

Yes, Your Honor.

CORA

Check in your patients.

DETMOLD

(*To* OLD LADY)
Your name, Madame?

OLD LADY

This doesn't fit. It's much too big. I wear a size eleven,
maybe a twelve—

DETMOLD

Did you always hate your father?

CORA

Convict her later, arrest her now! There's only one question
that needs answering.
      (*She sings*)
Are they breathing? Then they're Cookies.
Are they moving? Then they're Cookies.
Are they living? Then they're Cookies.
So get on with it! Quick, get on with it!
Are they human? Then they're Cookies.
So shut up, my dear Doctor, and shut her up too!
      (*The waltz ends with a flourish as the* OLD LADY *is
      clapped into the cage and the cage and the door
      slammed shut. A new waltz, a gentle one, begins and
      on dances—on point, of course—a* PILGRIM *we have
      seen before*)

CORA

      (*Sings*)
Lookie, lookie, here comes Cookie
Now.
Naughty Cookie, playing hookey—
That, we don't allow.
      (*Three* DEPUTIES *dance a pas de quatre with the*
      PILGRIM *who also is tossed into the cage at the end.
      Then other people are captured—waltz varia-
      tions—and locked up in the cage: a wildly weeping
      widow; a pair of young lovers; a "Blanche Du Bois."
      Finally, the activity is a bit too much for* CORA *who
      takes the key to the cage and hands it to* SCHUB—*who
      has just entered executing a* tour jeté—*as she sings*)

CORA

You take the key, my love,
I'm too exhausted to move!
Music, I must have music,
A moment's music or my head will burst!

(DEPUTIES *bring on her litter; a* QUARTET OF DEPUTIES
stands by it, ready to sing for her)

I know you'll meet the test—
You've been well rehearsed.
Do your best
(Meaning do your worst),
Let me rest
And remember, Schub-chen:
Women and children first!

(*She collapses on the litter. The* QUARTET *reprises*
"Lock 'Em Up" while SCHUB *does a variation with*
three different girls—whom he locks up. Now FAY
appears in her red wig and her red feather-trimmed
coat)

SCHUB

(*Speaks, to music*)

Not yet gone back to Lourdes yet?

FAY

Non

SCHUB

Pourquoi pas?

FAY

Pourquoi you hold ze key to my heart.

(*She whips out a feather fan and proceeds to do a*

wild ballroom waltz with SCHUB *during which she vamps him and gets the key out of his pocket. A* LADY DEPUTY *appears like an operatic soprano complete with chiffon handkerchief and trills madly while* FAY *pursues her task and gets rid of* SCHUB. FAY *then unlocks the cage and lets out the captured victims.* CORA *awakens from her little nap on the litter and is livid to find her victims gone. This inspires a furioso chase with* DEPUTIES *rounding up people wildly and dumping them in the cage.* CORA *goes off—Tally-Ho-ing for the hunt—at the moment when the* DEPUTIES *have captured a particularly fierce looking woman. They throw her in the cage but she escapes and proceeds to knock them out with a balletic series of spins, kicks and uppercuts. She stalks off and they are just coming to when* FAY *returns and sings frantically)*

FAY

Fire!
Hurricane!
Everyone off of ze streets!
Run for your lives! Run for your lives!
Ze dam has burst!
Run for your lives, run for your lives!
Ze lion's loose!
Fire, bubonic plague, air raid warning—
Hurry, run! Run! Run!

(*The clarion call is picked up by the frightened* DEPUTIES *who run about and off as* FAY *opens the cage and lets out the captured people. This time, they dance out like the swans in Swan Lake. The* DEPUTIES *return as the hunters in that ballet and a winding line of fleeing "Swans" led by* FAY *and following*

"Hunters" led by CORA *and* SCHUB *is dancing about the stage as the music builds to a big Tschaikovskian climax. The chase ends with a ballet tableau:* FAY *is downstage, stretched out in the arms of three* DEPUTIES; CORA *is to one side,* SCHUB *to the other.* DR. DETMOLD *ambles forward, looks down at* FAY *exactly as an analyst looks down on his patient)*

DETMOLD

Why, there you are, Nurse Apple! Have you been acting out your dreams?

CORA

Nurse Apple?? *(She reaches over and snatches off* FAY's *wig which she then hands to* SCHUB, *saying)* It's that Lady from Lourdes! I always knew she dyed her hair.

(The DEPUTIES *release* FAY *as* SCHUB *hands the wig to* MAGRUDER. *Other* DEPUTIES *roll the cage off and* HAPGOOD *appears on the balcony of the Hotel)*

SCHUB

(To FAY)

Dear lady, take defeat like a gentleman and hand over the records.

FAY

I don't have them.

CORA

(Indicating HAPGOOD)

Then he has!

FAY

No one has them.

CORA

How can no one have something that exists?

FAY

They don't exist. I destroyed them.

CORA

(*Indicating* FAY's *feather-trimmed coat*)
Magruder! Get out the tar! You can use her own feathers.

SCHUB

Haste makes waste, Madame President. (*To* FAY) The names will do. I'm sure you know them.

DETMOLD

By heart! She may never forget a face but she always remembers a name.

FAY

Oh, Dr. Detmold . . .

CORA

Front and center, missy.
        (*Slowly,* FAY *comes forward*)

HAPGOOD

(*Softly, in French*)
Courage, mademoiselle.

CORA

Never mind the *courage;* just the names.

FAY

I . . . I'll begin with the names of the people who faked the miracle.

SCHUB

What?!

FAY

Comptroller Schub and Mayor—

SCHUB

Anarchist!

COOLEY

Atheist!

CORA

Suffragette!

FAY

They invented the miracle! There's a pump in the old cave—

CROWD

Communist! Fascist! Red! Pink! Cheat! Liar! Fraud! Foreigner! Stoolpigeon! Embezzler! Capitalist! Egghead! Etc.
    (*They go for her but* HAPGOOD *leaps over the Hotel balcony and pulls* FAY *to one side, protecting her from*

the mob as SCHUB *orders the* DEPUTIES *to hold
them back)*

CORA

At ease . . . It's an old game for the fox to cry "wolf" when
she's really a rat. The names, Miss Apple, in alphabetical
order. Dr. Detmold, stand by to check in your homing pi-
geons.

> (FAY *stands alone. There is a slight movement from
> the crowd, as though some* COOKIES *are trying to
> hide)*

SCHUB

(Softly)
We are going to lock up forty-nine people, Nurse Apple.
Whether that includes the innocent—depends on a lady who
claims she fights for justice.

FAY

(After a moment)
Anthony, Susie B.
> (*A woman slowly comes forward*)
Brecht, Herman.
> (*A young man comes forward and stands next to the
> woman. During the following, others step out slowly
> and sadly, forming a column in two lines*)

FAY

Chaplin, Rodney . . . Dillinger, Myrna . . . Engels, Dave
. . . Freud, Harriet . . . Gandhi, Salvatore . . .
> (*Now she pauses a fraction longer.* HAPGOOD *looks at
> her, then steps forward and joins the column.* FAY
> *sees this and speaks hastily:*)
Ibsen, Selma . . .

(*At this,* HAPGOOD *leaves the line and walks up to* FAY. *But she turns away and continues to call other names as the lights dim and the "Bluebird" music begins softly*)

Jorgenson, Otto . . . Kierkegaard, Mac . . . Lafitte, Roger . . . Mozart, Miriam . . .

(*The stage is quite dim now. The brightest light is on the column of* COOKIES *as the grin breaks over their faces and they sing "The Bluebird Song" as they march off in the direction of Dr. Detmold's Cookie Jar.*

When the last note has trailed off, the stage is empty except for FAY *and* HAPGOOD. *Everyone else has disappeared into the darkness. She cannot face him, and his tone to her is cold*)

HAPGOOD

Why didn't you turn me in?

FAY

Why didn't you turn yourself in?

HAPGOOD

I can't stop being crazy. But that's my own affair.

FAY

No, it isn't. You're the hope of the world.

HAPGOOD

I don't think you can possibly repeat that sentence without laughing.

FAY

You're the hope of the world. You and all the crazy people like you.

HAPGOOD

From the first moment, you've been trying to put me on a white horse! Now stop it!

FAY

(*Turning to him, angrily*)
Then why don't you go turn yourself in now?!
(*A long moment; then*)

HAPGOOD

. . . I can't. And you know it. (*Then, with a smile*) Well, you might at least look pleased.

FAY

But now you'll go away.

HAPGOOD

You know, you confuse issues: you get too personal.

FAY

It's a problem ladies have.

HAPGOOOD

(*Goes to her*)
Come with me, Fay.

FAY

My Cookies need someone to take care of them.

HAPGOOD

That's an excuse. Come with me.

FAY

I'm too unmusical.

HAPGOOD

I'll teach you.

FAY

You tried that. You saw a minute ago how easily I crumble.

HAPGOOD

. . . Where's your wig?

FAY

You wouldn't want me like that. Not really. You see, you're
marvelous and crazy. I'm competent and practical—and that's
what *I'm* stuck with . . . But I'm very important here.
(*Music begins softly*)

HAPGOOD

Four wives: they all tried to change me. The girls who
don't . . . are the girls you don't marry.
(*He reaches out, almost touches her, then turns and
slowly starts off. But he stops as she begins to sing
very quietly*)

FAY

You like my hair, yes? My lips, yes?
Ze sway of my, how you say? of my hips . . .
Yes? . . .

(Music continues under; after a moment, she speaks)
You don't leave me with anything.

HAPGOOD

I'm sorry. For me, it was marvelous.

FAY

Marvelous?

HAPGOOD

(Sings)
With so little to be sure of,
If there's anything at all,
If there's anything at all,
I'm sure of her and now and us together.
All I'll ever be I owe you,
If there's anything to be.
Being sure enough of you
Makes me sure enough of me.
Thanks for everything we did,
Everything that's past,
Everything that's over too fast.
None of it was wasted,
All of it will last:
Everything that's here and now and us together!
It was marvelous to know you
And it isn't really through.
Crazy business this, this life we live in—
Don't complain about the time we're given—
With so little to be sure of in this world,
We had a moment!
A marvelous moment!

FAY

(Sings, quietly)

A marvelous moment.
A beautiful time.
I need you more than I can say.
I need you more than just today.
I guess I need you more than you need me,
And yet I'm happy.
All I'll ever be I owe you,
If there's anything to be.
Being sure enough of you
Made me sure enough of me.

HAPGOOD

(Simultaneously with the above)

The more I memorize your face,
The more I never want to leave.
Come with me, Fay.

FAY

(Shakes her head)

Thanks for everything we did,
Everything that's past,
Everything that's over too fast.

HAPGOOD

(Simultaneously)

There's more of love in me right now
Than all the little bits of love
I've known before.

BOTH

None of it was wasted,
All of it will last:

Everything that's here and now and us together!
It was marvelous to know you
And it's never really through.
Crazy business this, this life we live in—
Can't complain about the time we're given—
With so little to be sure of in this world—

FAY

(To herself)

Hold me.
Hold me.

> *(Softly, the music ends and they walk off in opposite
> directions, she toward the asylum, he toward the out-
> side world. The lights come up slowly on the town
> square and with them, comes the sound of bells peal-
> ing faintly in the distance. As the bells get louder and
> louder, first one, then another and another* PILGRIM
> *hurries excitedly across the square. Then a*
> TOWNSPERSON; *a* PILGRIM; *more* TOWNSPEOPLE; *all
> hurrying, excited, beckoning, all rushing elatedly to-
> ward the sound of the bells. During this,* CORA *rushes
> out of City Hall and tries to stop one of the running
> people)*

CORA

Where are you running? I asked you a question. You there,
with the blue pants with the pleats in front: WHERE ARE
YOU RUNNING? *(Calling into the doorway of City Hall)*
Cooley! Stop tampering with those books and find out what
that ringing is and what is—WHERE ARE YOU RUN-
NING? I am your Mayor-ess, Cora Hoover Hooper, and I
demand to know where—

COOLEY

(Outside now, beckons to one of the runners)
Ho there! Ho there!

CORA

"Ho there." Don't *ask,* you coward. Stop them; grab one of them; make one of them—(MAGRUDER *is racing by with a sexy young girl)* Magruder! MAGRUDER, STOP!

MAGRUDER

Excuse me, Y'r Honor—Brother Cooley—

CORA

Where are you running?

MAGRUDER

The town beyond the valley—they've got a miracle!

CORA

How dare they!

COOLEY

What's *their* water coming out of?

MAGRUDER

It ain't water. It's a miracle.

COOLEY

What do you mean, it's a miracle?

MAGRUDER

It's this statue—in the middle of the square—nothing and no one near it—and suddenly—it got a warm heart!

CORA

Oh, that can happen to anyone.

MAGRUDER

But this statue is made of marble! And they say a man who was born without sight just touched the heart of that statue and—

VELMA (The sexy girl)

(*To* Magruder)
Sam, are you coming? I wanna see that miracle today!

MAGRUDER

Okay, little lady. Excuse me, Y'r Honor, but maybe what ails me—
(*Backing away*)

VELMA

SAM!

MAGRUDER

Comin'!
(*He runs off with her*)

CORA

Magruder, you're disgusting and you're fired! (*To others fleeing*) You're all disgusting, and I'm going to fine everyone of you. Cooley! Cooley, where are you sneaking, you little sneak? Now don't tell me that you, of all people—

COOLEY

It could be a miracle.

CORA

It could not!

COOLEY

(*Hurrying off*)
I want to see for myself!

CORA

But if you've seen one, you've seen them all! Cooley! Cooley, you're fired! You there! I appoint *you* Treasurer! (*To another*) I appoint you Chief of Police! (*To another*) I appoint you (*But now her four* BOYS *come tapping across in an Off-to-Buffalo; and after them comes the rock as though even it wants to go to the new miracle.* CORA *calls desperately:*) SCHUB! COMPTROLLER SCHUB! Where are you? I need you! (*Silence. Everything stops. No more running, no more bells, and the rock is still behind her as* SCHUB *comes quietly out of City Hall. A moment*) Is it really you?

SCHUB

There is no reasonable facsimile of me.

CORA

And you're not running with the others?

SCHUB

My dear lady, running is for the herd. Come now, Cora: you can't win 'em all. You need to relax. Let's dine together this evening. My house at eight. Or your house. It makes no difference. I'll be at your house at seven.

CORA

(*Shakes her head*)
My lovely town. They'll be poor again and they'll hate me
again.

SCHUB

True.

CORA

I don't like economics, Schub. That's the trouble with making history. You come down from the mount or the hills: the
leader, the saviour. The peasants cheer and parade: "Off with
the old! On with the new!" It's all glamorous and exciting—
and then you have to get down to the dreary business of getting money in the till . . . Oh Schub, if only we could think
of a new miracle!

SCHUB

It isn't miracles we need, Cora. It's to be in step. Where's
everybody going? Mad.
(*He stops; she looks at him. Slowly, music comes in
under*)

CORA

(*Hushed*)
Schub—

SCHUB

Your Honor—

CORA

There's no more room at The Cookie Jar—

SCHUB

Your factories are empty—

CORA

Your houses are empty—

SCHUB

The stores are empty—

CORA

City Hall is empty—

SCHUB

Your Honor—

CORA

Schub—

SCHUB

We'll turn the whole damn town into a Cookie Jar!!!!

CORA

AND THEY'LL LOVE ME! (*Music: "I've Got You to Lean On." Very gay*) Schub, you *are* brilliant! If I'm not careful, I'll marry you.

SCHUB

It's your life or mine.

CORA

Mine. It's later than I thought.
   (*She sings*)
With you to depend on, I'll never quit.
There isn't a murder I couldn't commit.
Whenevcr I falter, Gibraltar comes through.
I've got you to lean on—
   (*A dance break*)

SCHUB

I've got you to lean on—
   (*A dance break*)

BOTH

I've got you to lean on—
   (*And on comes an official-looking woman in a severe
   suit, carrying a small black case. Her name is*
   OSGOOD)

OSGOOD

Excuse me, but could you direct me to The Cookie Jar?

CORA

Certainly! Right this way!
   (*And she and* SCHUB *dance off into City Hall.*
   OSGOOD *gapes at them as the music ends; and from
   across the square comes a small group of* COOKIES *led
   by* FAY *who is once again in her nurse's uniform*)

OSGOOD

Just a moment, nurse. Are you from Dr. Detmold's Asylum?

FAY

Yes, I'm the head nurse.

OSGOOD

Good, I'm Dr. Detmold's new assistant: Dr. Jane Borden Osgood.

FAY

I'm glad you're late.

OSGOOD

My train was delayed at the town beyond the valley. They have what they think is a miracle there.

FAY

Yes; we just heard.

OSGOOD

Well—hear—this! (*And the same music as for* FAY's *speech in the beginning comes in angrily*) Now—Point— One! I am a woman of science: control and order, reason and logic.

(*Slowly,* FAY *turns and stares at* OSGOOD *in horror*)

FAY

Oh, no!

OSGOOD

(*Simultaneously*)

I shall take these beings who are human on a quick march to that miracle, real or imaginary. If anyone of any race, creed, or color tries to stop you from taking that miracle, wait until you see the whites of their eyes and then spit—and spit *hard!* (*Music stops*) Human beings! Atten-shun! Forward— march! Hut-two-three-four! Hut-two-three-four!

> (*"The Bluebird Song" has come in as a loud, lusty march. Led by* OSGOOD, *the* COOKIES *march off to the new miracle, leaving* FAY *alone on the stage. She looks after them desolately, then murmurs*)

FAY

Oh, Hapgood . . . (*She moves, looking to where he last went off*) Hapgood? (*Frantically now, she climbs up the rock and calls desperately*) HAPGOOD! (*No answer, no sign*) HAPGOOD!!

> (*Nothing. She tries to whistle for him: not a sound. Then, she cups her hands around her mouth as though to shout for him but in one last, desperate effort, she shoves two fingers in her mouth and blows with all her strength and hope. And out comes a whistle: a shrill, piercing, ugly whistle—but it's a whistle! It even startles her but a great smile breaks over her face. A moment, then* HAPGOOD *saunters on*)

HAPGOOD

(*Laughing*)

That's good enough.

> (*The music of "With So Little to Be Sure Of" comes in strong as he lifts her down off the rock into his arms. They look at each other and kiss; and as they do, there is a surge of music from the orchestra and again, a great surge of water from the rock. But this time, it is an enormous spout of water which is every color of the rainbow and which drenches them like a shower as*

The Curtain Falls